POETIC VOYAGES
LEICESTERSHIRE VOL II

Edited by Simon Harwin

First published in Great Britain in 2002 by
YOUNG WRITERS
Remus House,
Coltsfoot Drive,
Peterborough, PE2 9JX
Telephone (01733) 890066

All Rights Reserved

Copyright Contributors 2001

HB ISBN 0 75433 482 1
SB ISBN 0 75433 483 X

FOREWORD

Young Writers was established in 1991 with the aim to promote creative writing in children, to make reading and writing poetry fun.

This year once again, proved to be a tremendous success with over 88,000 entries received nationwide.

The Poetic Voyages competition has shown us the high standard of work and effort that children are capable of today. It is a reflection of the teaching skills in schools, the enthusiasm and creativity they have injected into their pupils shines clearly within this anthology.

The task of selecting poems was therefore a difficult one but nevertheless, an enjoyable experience. We hope you are as pleased with the final selection in *Poetic Voyages Leicestershire Vol II* as we are.

CONTENTS

Asfordby Captains Close Primary School
Daniel Smith	1
Connor Franklin	1
Laura Fox	2
Charlotte Wright	2
Jamie Barratt	3
Jordan Dyer	3
Victoria Carter	4
Thomas Howell	4
Sarah Mostyn	5
Sam Haynes	5
Amanda Myles	6
Rachel Bailey	6
David Kemp	7
Richard Skeels	7
Edward Lightfoot	8
Chloe Barnard	8
Lucy Davies	9

Ashfordby Hill CP School
Kyle Robinson	9
Liam Simms	10
Claire Brown	10
Andrew Dunn	11
Charlotte Wright	12
James Brown	13
Lewis Dawson	14
Ben Wheeler	14
Emma Pickworth	15
Daniel Munton	15
Claire Freestone	16
Matthew Halliday	17
Naomi Peberdy	18

Brooke Hill Primary School

Dean Glover	19
Lewis Wakeford	19
Jemma Smith	20
Pippa Woodford	20
Rachel Baker	21
Luke Jackson	21
Thomas Reid & Edward Garden	22
Rosie Goddard	22
India Hamilton	23
Matthew Perry	23
Jessica Grammer	24
Antony Brown	24
Sian Kinal	25
Rebecca Williams	25
Andrew Lambert	26
Georgia Smith	26
Sophie Morgan	27
John Veasey & Daniel Talbott	27
Christopher Potter	28
Adam Parsons	28
Eliza Sheasby & Leah Gardner	29
Rosy Martin & Emma Brown	30
Georgia Gibson-Smith	30
Sophie Dale & Eliza Sheasby	31
Tom Harries	31
Laura Brown & Emily Duell	32
Hattie Hodgson & Amy Neville	32
Mica Palmer & Lillie Price	33

Church Langton Primary School

Laura Smith	33
Adam Mason	33
Caitlin McCole	34
Richard Kearvell-White	34
Bethany O'Callaghan	34
Jenna Robinson	35
James Smith	35

Oliver Brewin	35
Matt Hollis	36
Jess Slatter	37
Miles Barnes	37
Victoria Wright	38
Michaella Thorpe	38
Vickie Gillespie	39
Oliver Wilce	39
John Faye	40
Lauren Clayton	40
Victoria Reid	41
Robyn Jakeman	41
Eve Morley	42
Rebecca Drummond	42
Rachel Garton	42
Sabrina Higham	43
Carl Smith	43
Georgina Getliffe	43
Laura Scott	44
Ian McLauchlan	44
Heather Betts	45
David Pollard	45
Thomas Durno	45

Glenmere Primary School

Sophie Kozlowski	46
Ritchie Vincent	46
Sajid Kadri	47
Hannah Barnett	48
Danielle Wilson	48
Jessica Hayes	48
Hisham Chaudhary	49
Georgina Wills	49
Lewis Prendergast	50
Misha Penney	50
Daisy Dobrijevic	51

Great Bowden CE School
Alex Carpenter	51
Aaron Watts	52
Beth Dillon	52
Astrid Tooms	53
Lana Johnson	53
Sam Tyrell	54
Hannah Brittan	54
Amy Brewster	55
Michael McHugo	55
Kay Williams & William Bromley	55
Ruth Beacher	56
Aled Williams	56
Georgia John-Charles	57
James Sands	57

Great Dalby Primary School
Jonathan Millican	58
Jonathan Smith	58
Tiffany Hodges	59
Daniel Johnston	60
Mark Dixon	60
Laura Greaves	61
Sienna Brooks	61
Georgia Stevens	62
Anton Brookes	62
Payl Byrne	63
James Longden	63
Adam Houghton	64
Laura Baker	64
Jessica Collin	65
Catherine Bates	65
Grace Orgill	66
Lucy Fraser	67
Miranda Myers	68
Abigail Millican	68
Emily Fionda	69
Eli-Louise Lowe	70

Husbands Bosworth CE Primary School

Mark Lawton	70
Catherine Price	71
Gray Inman-Hall	71
Daniel Hickman	72
Joseph Day	72
Matthew Cartmell	73
Thomas Williams	73
Kelly Williamson	74
Jenny Begley	74
Stuart Wright	75
Sam McWilliam	75
Jessica Asher	76
Anna Leedham	76
Catherine Harvey	77
Jack Oliver	78

North Luffenham CE Primary School

Colin Mackellar	78
Kirsty Baines	79
John Reidy	79
Sarah Fallow	80
Natasha Schofield	80
Daniel Vincent	80
Oscar Dejardin	81
Abi Corby	81
Klaus Osterlund	81
Meredith Newby	82
Daniel Greetham	82
Natalie Morrison	83
Kirsty Everton	83
James Newsham	84
Chloe Thompson	84
Sophie King	85
Matthew Atkins	85
Andrew Williams	86
Matthew Turville	86
Anna Saunders	86

	Fergal Hainey	87
	Bianca Jantuah	87
	Andrew Sampson	88
Overdale Junior School		
	Lewis Farrow	88
	Aimee Noon	89
	Josh Smith	89
	Mary Goodhart	89
	Sophie Evans	90
	Jessica Archer	90
	Hend Ainine	91
	Hannah Sanderson	91
	Christopher Green	92
	Maya Lamoudi	92
	Rattan Flora	93
	Joseph Clowes	93
	Nicola Davis	94
	Jessica Sanders	94
	Ian Knibbs	95
	Carrieann	95
	Leighanne Holmes	96
	Harriet Pearson-Coe	96
	Beth Edwards	96
	Megan Hellmuth	97
	Edward Olszewski	97
	Emma Moore	97
	Rosie Tamhne	98
	Matthew Li	98
	Ashley Wright	99
	Alex Owczarek	99
	Joseph Little	100
	Naomi Bell	100
	Brooke Bradshaw	100
	Ashley Hagan	101
	Daniel Beaver	101
	Samuel James	101
	Chetan Mistry	102

Seema Saujani	102
Francesca White	102
Amit Gore	103
Bharante Mistry	103
Erica Goodwin	103
Emma Sainthouse	104
Nicola Hoy	104
Leah White	105
Stephanie Hinshaw	105
Rebecca Smith	106
Radhika Pabari	106
Mary James	107
Trish Munangi	107
Baljinder Sadhra	108
Ruby Cross	108
Richard Wale	109
Rehana Dyson	109
Meera Vithlani	110
Ayisha Mistry	110
Amanpreet Kaur Raja	110
Kenneth Lamb	111
Davey Martin-Hanley	111
Meera Gajjar	111
Gemma Collins	112
Cherith Johnston	113
Alice Lathbury	114
Lucy Smith	114
Michael Lanni	115
Asad Ahmed	115
Naomi Tugeman	116
Sebastian Owezarek	116
Sean Womersley	117
Amritpal Pooni	117
Chandni Thakrar	118
Renate McKenzie-Onah	118
Brendon Jones	119
Christina Meadows	119
Joseph Robinson	119

Manvir Rai	120

Ridgeway Primary School

Charlotte Clifford	120
Sam Robson	121
Nadine Panter	121
Jessica Bale	122
Nadine Weston	122
Luke Bishop	123
Katherine Berridge	124
Ryan Reed	124
Anand Patel	125
Liam Eyres	125
Christopher Liu	126
Kyle Lomer	127
Joseph Jeacock	128
Ryan March	128
Christopher Partridge	129
Alexandra Woodford	130
Emma Ritchie	130
Caroline Clayton-Drabble	131
Chloe Reynolds	132
Natalie Windle	132
Lewis Dyke	133
Hannah Twynham	134
Georgia Lewis	134
Liam Godlington	135
Daniel Plant	136
Brady Marlow	136
Gemma Smeeton	137
Matthew Gilbert	138
Adam Rippin	138
Charlotte Allen	139
Emily Beaulieu	140
Samantha Fulks	140
Charlotte King	141
Laura Moore	142
Jessica Wells	142

Chloe Martin	143
Sophie Barnett	143
Natasha Hepworth	144
Hannah Kilby	144
Dominic Reed	145
Kirstie Melville	146
Edward Crowe	146
Alice Learey	147
Toby Burbidge	148
Adam Parkins	148
Richard Sharman	149
Hannah Surkitt-Parr	150
Roxanne Gomez	151
Laura Brown	152
Nadine Dilley	153
Jamie Curzon	154
Jake Thompson	155
Abigail Jagoe	156
Nathan Saggers	156
Steven Jones	157
George Sykes	158
Hannah Williams	159
Sam Burgess	160
Joshua Allsop	161
Raphaelle March	162
Polly Underwood	163

St Mary's CE Primary School, Melton Mowbray

Bethany Gresley-Jones	163
Lauren Sinnott	164
Sara Hall	164
Annabelle Saxby	164
Megan Tymanskyj	165

The Grove Primary School

Ellie Stapleton	165
Sophie Agar	166
Jennifer Sharp	166

Lilith Dickinson	167
Hannah Tatnell	167
Amie-Leigh Claricoats	168
Catherine Bloxam	168
Gracie Ellam	169

The Poems

CATS

Cuddly, soft and furry
A cat is playful and climbs trees
Tears its claws through the settee
It stays where it lays by the fire
Cats are fun; cats are smart
Cats can see in the dark.
Their hair is as thick as a house wall.
Staring out the window frame
Acting like there is a storm.
Jumping up the wall so high,
Like it's going to touch the sky.
Cats are tired after a long day's walk,
So they go home and play with some chalk.

Daniel Smith (9)
Asfordby Captains Close Primary School

THE GOLDEN CHICKEN

Every time I go walking
I always see the golden chicken
He's always singing ringer ding-ding all day long.
When you next go he's always got eggs
You hear them hatching ting-a-ling ling,
All the ducks say quack-a-dack dack,
The next day the little chickens would have opened their eyes,
Then learnt the chicken song a-dong-dong.
So make sure when you see the golden chicken,
Sing the chicken song with him.

Connor Franklin (9)
Asfordby Captains Close Primary School

ME

I have many friends,
I am very kind,
I do plenty of work,
I have a helpful mind.

I love the colour lilac,
I don't like fish,
I like 'Friends' on TV,
I also don't like salt and vinegar crisps.

I like long, black, gleaming trousers,
I adore short mini skirts,
I love high, lilac shoes,
But I dislike blue shirts.

Laura Fox (11)
Asfordby Captains Close Primary School

ANIMAL

There once was a horse who ate tomato sauce.
There was a zebra named Debra.
Do elephants really eat ants?
There's a lizard in a blizzard.
The monkey was funky.
There was a seal who ate fish and chips for a meal.
The deer who drank beer.
There's a cat who wore a hat.
The pig who wore the wig to do the jig
And there's me who ate a flea!

Charlotte Wright (8)
Asfordby Captains Close Primary School

MY PET

My little pet went down the vet
And had a little pain
Because they checked his brain
So we went on holiday in a train
And on the way back we went on a plane
And when we got home (our dog had gone to bed) the light
                                                              was flashing
And the dog's tail was lashing
And when Mum was doing the cooking, the cooking was smoking
And the chicken was roasting
I got out of my bed
Then met my Uncle Fred
Had a sled.
My Uncle Fred said get your clothes on
Because we're going outside
Then we saw a plane fly.

Jamie Barratt (10)
Asfordby Captains Close Primary School

I HATE BULLIES

I hate bullies bossing people about, beating people up.
I hate bullies bullying people in football matches,
Kicking from behind because they don't dare to attack from the front
I think bullies are really wimps
They pick on people because they are different.
If you are being bullied just stand up for yourself,
Don't let bullies win.

Jordan Dyer (10)
Asfordby Captains Close Primary School

MY BEST FRIEND AMANDA

My best friend Amanda is like a cuddly panda.
She's very kind and nice,
She's even fair to mice,
She likes to play in the sand and make castles
So she hardly ever hassles,
Because she's a panda.
She likes bamboo and enjoys playing peep-a-boo,
Being best friends is hard,
But at Christmas we send each other a card.
Sometimes we fall out,
But we always work it out,
We fell out because we had a row but we're best friends again now,
She's as bright as the sun and likes eating a bun.
She's got a cat called Tigger,
Why I can never figure,
She likes to go out on her bike and ride and I know she'll always be
                                                          by my side.

Victoria Carter (9)
Asfordby Captains Close Primary School

FOX

The fox was calm as a sleeping cat
It became as angry as a roaring bear
A sharp wave.
As big as an ancient elephant
Stomp, stomp, bomp.
The fox zoomed off as speedy as a bullet
Bang, bang, boom
The fox was calm as a sleeping cat.

Thomas Howell (8)
Asfordby Captains Close Primary School

LUCY D

She's as cold as ice.
She's not scared of mice.
She wouldn't eat a fish
If it was left out on a little dish.
She's a best friend by a gust of wind
And would never say a word to hurt you.
She's like a newborn baby bunny
She's as kind as kind can be,
And she'll never leave you out.
She doesn't like sprouts,
And she'll never forget your secrets.
She's like a sparkling star glowing from the sky.
Like a big pizza pie
And she's still shining as bright
As she was up in the sky.
She's still silver and gleaming and sparkling, hopping
Like a big fat rabbit
And baby horse leaping through the sky,
She will never let you cry
As she's leaping through the sky.
It's Lucy Davis.

Sarah Mostyn (8)
Asfordby Captains Close Primary School

ANIMALS

The cat who wore a hat,
Spat when she had to tell the funky monkey
That the crazy, lazy lizard,
Is stuck in a blizzard with another lizard.

Sam Haynes (8)
Asfordby Captains Close Primary School

MY BEST FRIEND VICTORIA

My best friend Victoria has sparkly, pale, light blue eyes,
That glisten in the roasting sunlight,
And she is always right.

Victoria likes to call herself Tory,
Often in games she's a dog called Cory,
We sometimes fall out,
But we always work it out.

Being best friends is hard,
It's like trying to stand up on greasy lard.

We fell out because we had a row,
But we're best friends again now.

Amanda Myles (9)
Asfordby Captains Close Primary School

THE SEA

The sea looked like an amazing, dark, cloudy sky,
Crashing against the cold, bleak moor
Waiting to turn into an extensively huge storm.

The sea sounded like a roaring lion hunting for its prey,
Clashing against the foam on the snowy mountains.

The sea moved as quickly as a leaping lemur guarding its prey,
Seeing it as a big wave crashing onto the deserted beach.

Rachel Bailey (10)
Asfordby Captains Close Primary School

DREAMS

Dreams can be happy
With lots of chocolates
And new friends to play with.

Dreams can be scary
With zombies and blood.

Dreams can be sad
Like losing a toy
Or someone dying.

Dreams can be exciting
With holidays and Christmas
Or Easter dreams.

David Kemp (8)
Asfordby Captains Close Primary School

I DREAM OF . . .

I dream of a pot of gold at the end of a rainbow,
I dream of skiing down a steep hill,
I dream of a sparkling summer sun,
I dream of flying without wings,
I dream of going on an adventure that never ends,
I dream of gardens made of clouds,
I dream of sailing on the deep seas,
I dream of being a millionaire.

Richard Skeels (9)
Asfordby Captains Close Primary School

THE SNAKE

The snake was as angry as elephants hitting against each other
The snake was smelling for scrummy prey
It was as fast as a cheetah at full pelt
The snake could smell his prey over one metre away
Over a hill nearby.
The snake was rushing through the jungle
His skin was bouncing off the sun
The sound of a snake could be heard for miles away
It seemed that it was making the ground shake
Swaying side by side.
The snake carried a sssssss noise
The weather was as angry as a cheetah who just missed his prey
The snake went away.

Edward Lightfoot (8)
Asfordby Captains Close Primary School

CHIMPANZEE

C rafty chimpanzee,
H appy as they swing from tree to tree,
I ts fur all black
M um clinging on to her young,
P recious babies, very small,
A dventures of chimpanzees,
N aughty, cheeky chimpanzees
Z any personality,
E yes dark brown,
E ars are little petals.

Chloe Barnard (9)
Asfordby Captains Close Primary School

Dogs

Dogs have very big paws,
And if you look they have big jaws,
They won't go to sleep,
The poor dog snores.

Lucy Davies (9)
Asfordby Captains Close Primary School

The Magic Box

I will put in my box . . .
The rain splashing on the windowpanes,
My mum's cooking that is lovely,
And the sniff of a brand new comic book.

I will put in my box . . .
The seeds of a growing plant,
A flicker of light as I press the switch,
And a baby bird flying in the sky.

I will put in my box . . .
The fire of the blazing sun,
The smoke from the chimney on a cold winter's day,
And the coolness of the chilly moon.

I will put in my box . . .
The falling conkers of the horse chestnut tree,
Falling leaves in the autumn,
Lambs in the field in the spring,
And cool water on my feet as I paddle in the sea.

I will jump in my box and look at the crystal clear top.

Kyle Robinson (10)
Asfordby Hill CP School

THE MAGIC BOX

I will put in my box . . .
The rain clashing on a white wash fence,
A snowy winter's morning,
A warm pleasant summer evening.

I will put in my box . . .
A field full of golden daffodils,
The biggest mansion,
And one animal.

I will put in my box . . .
A river of peace,
A mountain so high,
And a sandy desert,
Full of quiet.

My box is made of crocodile skin
Hinges made from frogs' legs,
And no lock
Just two lions to guard.

Liam Simms (10)
Asfordby Hill CP School

THE MAGIC BOX

I will put in my box . . .
The romantic aroma of pot pourri,
The strawberry flavour of wobbly jelly,
And the beautiful smell of freshly baked bread.

I will put in my box . . .
The warm, melted wax of a burnt candle,
The cuddly feeling of a kitten's fur,
And the cold sensation of cubes of ice.

I will put in my box . . .
The noisy popping of bubble wrap,
The soft feeling of a baby's skin,
And the squeaking of dolphins in the bright blue sea.

Claire Brown (11)
Asfordby Hill CP School

THE MAGIC BOX

I will put in my box . . .
The whack of a whimpering wallaby,
Six stacks of sticky stew,
A box of stale bread from Egypt.

I will put in my box . . .
A ripple from a passing wave,
A howl from a rushing rhino,
Three chopsticks from the Chinese takeaway.

I will put in my box . . .
Four giraffes leaping high in the air,
The wisest teacher,
The most forgetful elephant.

My box is made from silk,
Stretched with silver aluminium and pure gold.
My box has colourful rainbows
And the hinges are made from freshly baked gingerbread.

I shall fly in my box,
Through cotton wool clouds,
Into the red, fiery sunset
Then glide through glittering jewels,
To watch the silver moon.

Andrew Dunn (10)
Asfordby Hill CP School

THE MAGIC BOX

I will put in the box . . .
The trot, trot of the horse's hooves on the road,
Fresh fruit found on a fruit tree,
Your feet in the first fallen snow.

I will put in the box . . .
A bowl of ice cream,
A cup of water from Australia
The last hair on a bald man's head.

I will put in the box . . .
Two wishes to a genie from me,
The first walk of a foal,
The last walk of a person.

I will put in the box . . .
A summer flower straight from the ground,
A tiger in a tutu,
A ballerina in stripes.

My box is fashioned from gold and fluff,
With ponies on the lid and stars in the corners,
Its hinges are the hind legs of a hound dog.

I shall run in my box,
On the highest mountain there is
Then I shall jump and land on a beach full of animals.

Charlotte Wright (11)
Asfordby Hill CP School

THE CASTLE OF SOUNDS

Clattering . . .
The rusty shutters slamming into each other.
Shattering . . .
The cracked pots being thrown by mischievous invisible hands.
Howling . . .
A fleaed-up werewolf entrapped in a rat infested dungeon.
Growling . . .
A three-headed gargoyle springing to life.
Moaning . . .
The ancient ghouls crying for blood-red revenge.
Groaning . . .
An old prisoner begging an axe man for mercy.
Clashing . . .
The blood-stained swords of two battling, decapitated horsemen.
Bashing . . .
An invisible hand hitting piano keys.
Creaking . . .
The dry rot floorboards which have seen better days.
Squeaking . . .
The voice of a young boy waiting for his mum.
Tickling . . .
The dilapidated grandfather clock chiming midnight all the time.
Clicking . . .
The rotting door trapping me into a dark room.

All to be heard in the castle of sounds.

James Brown
Asfordby Hill CP School

THE MAGIC BOX

I will put in my box . . .
The sound of a streaking air raid bomb,
Fire from a rotten, burnt house,
The tip of a cane torturing someone.

I will put in my box . . .
The silver sparkly waterfall,
With a see-through diamond ball,
The twinkling stars high in the sky.

I will put in my box . . .
A spaceman deep in the ocean
The deep sea diver high in outer space,
With a shooting star shining so bright.

My box looks like an ordinary box
Because all the specials are inside.

Lewis Dawson (10)
Asfordby Hill CP School

ANGER!

Anger is when you can't stay in bed on a Monday morning.

Anger is when you go swimming and you've forgotten your trunks.

Anger is when you find out that you've got sour milk on your cereals.

Anger is when someone's put a coffee stain on your recently
                                          finished homework.
(Someone's in trouble!)

Anger is a way of life . . . and mmm . . . coffee is!

Ben Wheeler (11)
Asfordby Hill CP School

IF I WAS THE QUEEN OF ENGLAND

If I was the Queen of England I would . . .
Get more alarms and cameras for banks,
And get rid of all war tanks.

If I was the Queen of England I would . . .
Make sure the trees don't get cut down,
And then visit every town.

If I was the Queen of England I would . . .
Try and do my best to make a difference,
And homes for no rent.

If I was the Queen of England I would . . .
Clean oil spillages in the rivers, seas and oceans
And get dead people's lives (if relatives do not mind).

Emma Pickworth (11)
Asfordby Hill CP School

CASTLE OF SOUNDS

Clanking . . .
The drawbridge dropping as the headless horseman gallops in.
Spanking . . .
The rotten window shutters colliding with the window frame.
Snapping . . .
Crocodiles surfacing, waiting until their prey enters.
Tapping . . .
The zombies stumbling down the ancient corridor.
Groaning . . .
An entrapped werewolf in a vampire bat infested torture chamber.
Moaning . . .
A mummy locked in a haunted elevator.

Daniel Munton (10)
Asfordby Hill CP School

THE CASTLE OF SOUND

Creaking,
The rotten floorboards as a zapped zombie stalks slowly over them.
Squeaking,
The brave mice in a rusty deep, dark, dangerous cellar.
Smashing,
The glasses dropping out of a rotten one hundred year old cupboard.
Crashing,
The rusty, dusty castle locks down in the ditches.
Weeping,
A spider infested werewolf locked in a deep, dark dungeon.
Creeping,
Poor men begging the zombie for francs.
Ticking,
The rotten grandfather clock tocking.
Clicking,
The spooky animals running up drain pipes.
Crumbling,
The paper rustling by the door crisply.
Mumbling,
Old people whispering beneath their breath silently.
Tapping,
Vampires and Frankenstein knocking on the worm infested door.
Snapping,
Bulldogs biting dangerous tabby cats.
Banging,
Animals scratching the windows to wake fatso ghost.
Clanging,
The rusty drawbridge lifts up.

Claire Freestone (10)
Asfordby Hill CP School

THE MAGIC BOX

I will put in my box . . .
The poison of the pumping petrol,
Water from tusks of a huge African elephant,
The bits of the crumbly chocolate cake.

I will put in my box . . .
A scarecrow that always says boring,
A swig of the golden beer,
A flash of the dazzling fireworks.

I will put in my box . . .
Soft singing from the tuneful birds,
The spectacular sunrise,
And the moon's shadow across the lake.

I will put in my box . . .
An eighth wonder of the world and a man on Mars,
A clown in a bull ring,
And a bull in the circus.

My box is glowing like a red hot sunbeam,
With sequins all over the sides, corners and lid
Its hinges like a gigantic mouth of the alligator.

I shall row in my box,
On a massive tidal wave,
Over the ocean blue,
Then float ashore to a treasure island
Full of diamonds and gold.

Matthew Halliday (10)
Asfordby Hill CP School

My Magic Box

I will put in my box . . .
The wham of wizard's wand on a winter day
Licking up the crumbs where the cake lay
The dark rushing clouds like a water spray.

I will put in my box . . .
My favourite character from a book,
A snippet of a four leafed clover's luck
The first ever quack of a baby duck.

I will put in my box . . .
The very best words spoken in Latin,
The first ever threads of silky satin,
The last sound of a dog pantin'.

I will put in my box . . .
A second summer and a blue sea,
A hive with a bouncy flea,
And a dog with a buzzing bee.

My box is full of warmth - yet icy cold
The outside is shiny, solid gold
It is very young, yet anciently old.

I will keep my box for miserable times
Because in my box I will find
A world where everyone is kind
And full of a peaceful happy mind.

Naomi Peberdy (11)
Asfordby Hill CP School

FIRST SPORT

'Mum, can I have a new coat?'
'What about a football?'
'No, just a coat please.'
'What about football boots?'
'No, just a coat please.'
'What about trainers?'
'No, just a coat please.'
'What about a Liverpool kit?'
'No, just a coat please.'
'What about a new hat?'
'No, just a coat please.'
'Are you sure you don't want anything else?'
'No, I only want a coat please.'
'OK then get the one you want.
What! One hundred and forty pounds?
You can't have that.'
'Pleassssseeeeeee.'

Dean Glover (11)
Brooke Hill Primary School

ARNOLD BLITS WHO HAD MEGA FITS

There once was a boy called Arnold Blits
Who kept on having mega fits.
One day bubbles came out of his top
After that his head went pop!
Poor little Arnold started to melt
You can just imagine how everyone felt!

Lewis Wakeford (8)
Brooke Hill Primary School

ANIMALS

What is a cat?
A big furry thing.
What is a dog?
A licking machine.
What is a hamster?
It stores food in its mouth.
What is a fish?
It swims high and low.
What is a monkey?
Something that climbs trees.
What is a fox?
A very fast animal.
What is a horse?
Something you ride.
What is a cow?
A milking machine.
What is a zebra?
It's a road crossing.

Jemma Smith (11)
Brooke Hill Primary School

A CAUTIONARY TALE

There was a child called Samuel Lones
Who ate nothing except very sharp bones.
He loved the bones of both sheep and goats
And sadly one got stuck in his throat.
He gasped for breath as he sat alone
But nobody heard his last long moan.

Pippa Woodford (8)
Brooke Hill Primary School

ANCIENT GREECE

Ancient chocolate, ancient book, ancient France -
Oh, ancient Greece
Why, oh why ancient Greece?
Medusa, Minotaur, Hydra, Golden Fleece
Why so many characters?
Oh, it's boring ancient Greece.
Athens, Spartan, Troy, Marathon
Boring ancient Greek cities,
Found in ancient Greece.
Zeus, Aphrodite,
Hera, Poseidon
Why so many gods?

Because it's ancient Greece.

Rachel Baker (7)
Brooke Hill Primary School

SPACE

Space is where aliens love to play,
That's what people on Earth like to say.
Saturn has a ring,
As golden as spring.
Pluto is small,
And shaped like a ball.
Mars is for Martians,
You approach them with caution.
Venus is icy and cold,
That's what people on Earth have been told.

Luke Jackson (9)
Brooke Hill Primary School

THE SPORTS SHOP

'Excuse me, please can I have a golf club?'
'Purple or red?'
'Purple please.'
'Blue or orange?'
'No just a purple one please.'
'What about three clubs sir?'
'No just one, make it quick.'
'Long or short?'
'Short please and hurry up.'
'Do you want a trolley to go with it?'
'I might as well.'
'Only £100.'
'£100, what!'
'OK £200'
'Fine.'

Thomas Reid (10) & Edward Garden (11)
Brooke Hill Primary School

THE WITCH'S KITCHEN

Smells drift through the door and pans cracked on the floor,
Sneaking rats zoom across the kitchen tiles,
Spells bubbled inside the cauldron,
Spiders jumped from web to web,
Screeching bats flew and flew,
Spell books spread all round the room,
And witch's hats spin round and round
Until the witch comes along and every thing goes back to normal.

Rosie Goddard (8)
Brooke Hill Primary School

ANIMAL ANTICS

Tigers leap,
Hamster sleep.

Kangaroos hop,
Horses clop.

Fish swish,
Unicorns wish.

Parrots squawk,
Hens walk.

Worms squiggle,
But I wriggle.

India Hamilton (9)
Brooke Hill Primary School

TEACHER, TEACHER PLEASE!

Teacher, teacher please!
Let me have a piece of cheese.
Please, please I want lunch,
Can I join in that great bunch?
I need some paper, yes I do,
And teacher I also need the loo.
What am I doing teacher?
I really want some pizza, please
I need that piece of great big cheese
Oh please teacher, I need that cheese,
Please!

Matthew Perry (7)
Brooke Hill Primary School

MY TRAIN JOURNEY

The train rushed by, clickety clack,
The trees all a blur,
Rushing along to the destination,
Children chattering,
Pencils clattering,
Rushing past villages,
Houses blurring in the distance,
Slowing down,
Getting off,
Carrying on,
Doing puzzle books,
Playing snap with cards,
Slowing down again,
I get off,
What a busy train journey.

Jessica Grammer (9)
Brooke Hill Primary School

THE WITCH'S KITCHEN

In the witch's kitchen you can hear black cats purring
There's a table with a cauldron sitting on it,
You can see a broomstick leaning against the old dusty cupboard,
There's a dusty grandfather's clock ticking away,
You can smell stale air,
There are spiders webs hanging from the ceiling,
There are frogs hopping and croaking,
There is a book of spells and a witch's hat floating in the air,
There are potions frothing out of the cauldron.

Antony Brown (9)
Brooke Hill Primary School

CAN I HAVE A MILKSHAKE?

'Can I have a milkshake?'
'Cappuccino, coffee or tea?'
'Can I have a milkshake?'
'The lemonade's very nice.'
'Can I have a milkshake?'
'What about a beer or are you driving?'
'Can I have a milkshake?'
'The orange juice is fresh today.'
'Can I have a milkshake?'
'With or without rum?'
'Can I have a milkshake *please*?'
'Sorry sir but we're closed today!'

Sian Kinal (11)
Brooke Hill Primary School

CAN YOU GUESS WHAT IT IS?

Fat belly,
Not smelly,
Wagging tail,
Scared of hail,
Strong and hairy back,
Pink but can be black,
Loves food,
Bad or good mood,
Loves straw,
A bit like a boar,
Can you guess what she is?
She's Shelly, a pig.

Rebecca Williams (10)
Brooke Hill Primary School

AT THE SPORTS SHOP

'Tennis racket, squash racket, a cricket bat?'
'None of that!
Just some trainers.'
'Football boots, cricket trousers, a rugby top?'
'Stop!
Just some trainers please.'
'Cricket helmet, a gum shield, shin pads?'
'No I use Dad's.
Just some trainers please.'
'Football, rugby ball, golf ball?'
'Not at all.
Just some trainers please.'
'Leicester kit, Liverpool kit, Man Utd. Kit?'
'In a minute I'll have a fit!
Just some trainers please!'
'A basketball, a basketball post, a hockey stick?'
'Are you thick?
Just some trainers please!'
'Why didn't you say so before?'

Andrew Lambert (11)
Brooke Hill Primary School

BIRD FLIGHT

High, high in the sky
Day has broken, time to fly
High up in the sky.

Georgia Smith (11)
Brooke Hill Primary School

AT THE SUPERMARKET

'Now madam, what would you like?
Some fancy balloons or a brand new bike?'
'No just some milk please.'
'Crisps by the packet or if you say
A bottle of wine that goes off in May?'
'No just some milk please.'
'Lamb that's just come in,
Or a bottle of our finest gin?'
'No just some milk please.'
'Or take the pizza, it's succulent, very nice,
Or take the spicy peppers mixed in with spice.'
'No just some milk please.'
'Ahhh! Just some cream, it's top in the charts
Or a pack of twelve strawberry tarts?'
'*No* just some milk *please*.'
'Milk? Why didn't you say?
It's over here, this way,
Now would you like semi-skimmed, it's number ten?'
'Oh no! Here we go again!'

Sophie Morgan (10)
Brooke Hill Primary School

WATERFALL

Splashing on the rocks
Wonderful blue waterfall
Drifting into mist.

John Veasey & Daniel Talbott (11)
Brooke Hill Primary School

OWLS

Milky-white,
Very bright,
Spotted-brown,
On their crown,
Expert-hunters,
Don't like punters,
Sharp claws,
Don't have jaws,
Night-hooters,
Vermin-looters,
Stealthy-flyers,
Don't need tyres.
Born-keepers,
Rough-sleepers,
Mice-catchers
Nightly-snatchers,
Snow-likers,
Feather-givers,
They never growl.
It's an owl.

Christopher Potter (11)
Brooke Hill Primary School

THUMPER

Thumper is my rabbit,
He likes to run and play.
He's always getting up to something
Every single day.

He always gets excited
When I come home from school.
He jumps around and thumps his feet,
Really loses his cool.

Thumper is black all over,
His chest as white as snow,
His feet are as big as hammerheads
And his eyes say 'Hello.'

His ears are long and floppy
I love them very much,
They are so soft and warm
For me to stroke and touch.

Adam Parsons (10)
Brooke Hill Primary School

AT THE CORNER SHOP

'Hello my dear!
How nice of you to come down here,
Now, what would you like?
A loaf of bread or some freshly caught pike?'
'No, just six eggs please.'
'A slice of ham?
Some coke in a can?'
'No, just six eggs please.'
'Apple strudels?
Some Chinese noodles?'
'No, just six eggs please.'
'Three bags of peas?
A half of cheese?'
'No, just six eggs please.'
'Fairy liquid, a bottle of Squeeze?
A tub of humbugs, would go down easy?'
'No, just six eggs please.'
'You should have said earlier my dear
We really are quite busy in here.'

Eliza Sheasby (11) & Leah Gardner (10)
Brooke Hill Primary School

It's A ...

Night-time keeper,
Daytime weeper,
Bottle sucker,
Nappy mucker,
One huge burp,
Followed by a slurp,
First dummy,
First word 'Mummy',
A cuddly bear,
Single strand of hair,
It only crawls
But mainly bawls,
It's a ...

Rosy Martin & Emma Brown (11)
Brooke Hill Primary School

I Have A Friend

I have a friend who is good at drawing,
I have a friend who likes to sing,
I have a friend who writes very neatly,
I have a friend who likes to talk a lot,
I have a friend who makes me laugh,
I have a friend who never gets on with her work,
I have a friend who talks very loudly,
I have a friend who is afraid of nearly everything,
I have a friend ...

Georgia Gibson-Smith (10)
Brooke Hill Primary School

GUESS WHO?

Silent-swimmer,
Deadly-killer,
Teethy-grin,
Everything goes in,
Silver-scare,
With no hair,
Long and clever,
Skin like leather,
Haunts the dark,
It's a . . . shark!

Sophie Dale (10) & Eliza Sheasby (11)
Brooke Hill Primary School

IT'S A MOOOOOOOO

Multicoloured milkshake,
Makes a very nice steak,
Grass-hoover,
Slow-mover,
Bull-lover,
Seat-cover,
It's black and white,
And it's not very light,
If you haven't got it by now,
I'd better tell you
It's a Moooooooo.

Tom Harries (11)
Brooke Hill Primary School

SHE IS . . .

Golden-locked,
Well-frocked,
Groovy-dancer,
Rhythmic-prancer,
Fast-runner,
She's a stunner,
Netball-centre,
Lucy's lent her,
A Playstation game,
But what's her name?

Laura Brown & Emily Duell (10)
Brooke Hill Primary School

ROLLER COASTER HAIKU

Up the scary slope
Down the horrifying track
Round the loop-the-loop.

Whizzing upside down
Through the rickety tunnel
Screaming all the way.

Ahhhhhhhh!

Hattie Hodgson (10) & Amy Neville (9)
Brooke Hill Primary School

A Haiku About A Ghost

Floating through the sky,
Haunting everyone nearby,
White as the snow fall.

Mica Palmer (11) & Lillie Price (10)
Brooke Hill Primary School

I'd Like To Paint . . .

I'd like to paint the smell of home-made bread,
  The feel of happiness.
I'd like to paint the touch of frost,
  The coldness of snow.
I'd like to paint the feel of freedom,
  And the touch of caring.

Laura Smith (10)
Church Langton Primary School

Pandora

She is the sunset purple
The sound of soft drum beats
Thunder and lightning
Winter is she.

Adam Mason (9)
Church Langton Primary School

PANDORA

She is a mysterious purple,
The most hideous scorpion,
She is the black plague,
The key to Hell,
She is love decaying,
Suffering and grief is her shadow.

Caitlin McCole (10)
Church Langton Primary School

THE SUN

Brightly shines the sun
Watching over the Earth
Giving us life and making things grow
Its warmth envelops like a loving hug.

Richard Kearvell-White (11)
Church Langton Primary School

I'D LIKE TO PAINT...

The smell of a newborn baby,
The magic of paradise,
The feeling of softness,
The power of love,
The gentleness of friendship,
The wonders of mankind.

Bethany O'Callaghan (10)
Church Langton Primary School

PANDORA

She is mysterious purple
Like a high note on a piano.
She is a winner of all wars,
She is a flash of lightning,
She is a loud rocket,
She is a gloomy spider crawling around.

Jenna Robinson (10)
Church Langton Primary School

SPACE

Lifeless,
Eternity,
Mystical, magical,
Floating secret wonderful worlds,
Orbit.

James Smith (11)
Church Langton Primary School

I'D LIKE TO PAINT . . .

The taste of freshly baked bread,
The sound of newly born lambs,
The smell of freshly cut hay,
The coldness of snowflakes,
The softness of a newly born calf's coat.

Oliver Brewin (10)
Church Langton Primary School

GOOD HOPE

After Benjamin Zephania.

I have a dream of a clean world,
Where there is no pollution
And where we can all breath pure air.

I believe . . .
One day good will triumph
And we can live in unison forever.

I believe . . .
Religion should not be an issue
We are all the same inside
And that we can work and play
In peace and harmony.

I believe . . .
Poverty can stop
And all will be equal.

I believe . . .
We can cure illness,
Stop the world's greatest killer
And stay in perfect health.

This can happen
I know it can,
I believe in you,
Believe in me!

Matt Hollis (10)
Church Langton Primary School

CHARGE OF THE TOT BRIGADE

Half a toddle, half a toddle
Half a toddle onward
Into the big playground
Toddled the six hundred.

'Forward the tot brigade!
Grab hold of the big ones!' he said
'Capture year six!' he said
Onward they waddled
Legs to the right of them,
Legs to the left of them,
Screams unnumbered
Aghh! - through the basketball hoop
Raided the bins for food
Captured the big playground
Thanks to the tot brigade,
Dribbling six hundred!

Jess Slatter (10)
Church Langton Primary School

WINTER

Winter creeps unnoticed once more
Tormenting the Earth with wind and snow,
It grips the world with icy fingers
From its cold breath granite statues form
Until the resurrection of the sun.

Miles Barnes (11)
Church Langton Primary School

THE CHARGE OF THE BABE BRIGADE

Half a run, half a run,
Half a run onward
Into the cafeteria
Ran the six hundred.

Forward the babe brigade
'Charge for the sausages' they screamed
'Capture the chips' shouted another.
Onward they ran
Food to the left of them,
Food to the right of them,
Running babes unnumbered.

Victoria Wright (10)
Church Langton Primary School

PANDORA

She is the shade of sundown purple,
The top E of a violin,
She is a bolt of jagged lightning,
A clap of thunder,
The phantom from a nightmare,
The winner of all wars,
Sent to spoil human happiness,
Sent to devastate the Earth.

Michaella Thorpe (10)
Church Langton Primary School

CHARGE OF THE COW BRIGADE

Half a chew, half a chew,
Half a chew onward
Into the farmyard
Charged the six hundred.

Forward the cow brigade
'Find our passports' he said
'Capture the trailers' he said
Onward they thundered
Sticks to the right of them,
Sticks to the left of them,
Hands unnumbered.
Crunch through the new bails of hay
Shattering their trailer ranks
'Capture their cheque books'
Thanks to the cow brigade
Noble six hundred.

Vickie Gillespie (11)
Church Langton Primary School

DAWN

Scurrying across the dark lawn
Under clouds of a raging storm
Sees birds upon golden trees.
Branches blown by a cool winter's breeze
As they see the break of dawn
The ice starts to melt on the silvery lawn.

Oliver Wilce (11)
Church Langton Primary School

CHARGE OF THE TORY BRIGADE

Half a Hague, half a Hague,
Half a Hague onward
All in the Houses of Parliament
Sat the six hundred.

Bring on the elections!
'Charge for the ballot box' he cried
Voting to the right of them,
Voting to the left of them,
'Capture the votes!' he said
Crash through to No. 10!
Shatter their reputation!
Seize the seats
Tories celebrate
Governing six hundred.

John Faye (10)
Church Langton Primary School

THE DEATH

Sadness clutched me,
It was impossible to see.
No one understood,
No one ever would.
And when I remembered you
I realised there was nothing I could do.
    I wish you were here,
    I wish you were near.

Lauren Clayton (10)
Church Langton Primary School

THE CHILD BRIGADE

Half a child, half a child
Half a child onward
Into the valley of teachers
Rode the six hundred.

Forward the child brigade
'Charge for the books' he said
'Capture the books' he said,
Onward they clambered.
Teachers to the right of them,
Teachers to the left of them,
Shouted and thundered,
Crash through the teacher's door,
Don't let them bore you anymore,
Capture the books,
Hold the books hostage,
Say thanks to the child brigade,
The heroic six hundred.

Victoria Reid (11)
Church Langton Primary School

FROST

Quickly, quietly sneaks the frost,
The plants in the garden now lost.
Seconds later, has come the cold,
And soon after taken its hold.
The frost is a deathly white,
And seizes everything in sight.

Robyn Jakeman (11)
Church Langton Primary School

WINTER

Winter's elegant work
Creates non-enduring art
Which dies gracefully.

Needle and thread in
Hand she casts her gowns around cold
Despairing townsfolk.

Eve Morley (9)
Church Langton Primary School

ANGER

Anger stalked its prey
Its victim unsuspecting
It pounced with venom.

Rebecca Drummond (11)
Church Langton Primary School

SPRING

With new golden hands
Spring shakes the desperate earth
Out of its grey gloom.

Weary, worried worlds
She gradually takes her turn
Caressing icy earth.

Rachel Garton (11)
Church Langton Primary School

I'D LIKE TO PAINT . . .

I'd like to paint the touch of a new spring day,
The magic of the snow,
The sound of the ocean,
The taste of lost words.

Sabrina Higham (9)
Church Langton Primary School

WINTER

Winter's eyes searching
Looking for old November
Having no success.

But is he hidden?
There he is lurking in leaves
Every street freezing.

Carl Smith (9)
Church Langton Primary School

I'D LIKE TO PAINT . . .

I'd like to paint the touch of frost,
    The sound of waves crashing.
I'd like to paint the feeling of my dog's wet tongue,
    The taste of jam doughnuts.
I'd like to paint the cry of winter,
    The magic of the rainforest.

Georgina Getliffe (9)
Church Langton Primary School

AUTUMN VS WINTER

Winter searches for
Autumn footsteps in the snow
But he is nowhere.

Every alley and street
Is covered in snow and ice
Where is autumn now?

Autumn is hiding
In the leaves he's defeated
Winter's here to stay.

Winter senses the
Coming of spring and summer
But where is winter now?

Laura Scott (9)
Church Langton Primary School

PANDORA

She is sunset purple,
She is the trumpet of death,
A tunnel of darkness is she.
She is a boom of thunder,
She is a curious cat about a bulging box,
A crash of a drum is she.
She is tormented by temptation,
A seeker of secrets is she.

Ian McLauchlan (10)
Church Langton Primary School

ARIADNE

Graceful,
Maiden of peace,
Spirit of happiness,
Admirable lady of love,
Pure joy.

Heather Betts (10)
Church Langton Primary School

PANDORA

She is the foolish hero of evil,
She is the screech of the flute,
The tornado circling day and night.
She is the vulture of the box,
She is the demolition ray,
The cracked jewel,
The wandering spider is she.

David Pollard (10)
Church Langton Primary School

WHAT IS SNOW?

Snow is feathers from an angel's pillow.
Snow is sugar sprinkled from Heaven.
Snow is cotton wool floating from God's bedroom.
Snow is a soft covering of diamonds.

Thomas Durno (9)
Church Langton Primary School

THE COTTAGE ON THE LITTLE HILL

There is a cottage on a little hill,
My dad's name is big bad Bill.
The cottage on the little hill,
Is by a farmer's windmill.

There is a cottage on a little hill,
My mum is called kind, caring Jill.
We moved out of
The little house on the hill.

We are missing Jack and Jill.
My little brother is called cheeky Jack,
But hey,
Everybody might be moving back!

We have moved back,
And I am happy.
My mum has had a baby,
And I hate to smell the nappy!

Sophie Kozlowski (8)
Glenmere Primary School

THE BIRD THAT CAN'T FLY

Once there was a bird, a bird that couldn't fly
He can't even fly when he's had a pie.
A pie is his favourite food, he eats it every day,
And when he feels sleepy, he sleeps on a bundle of hay.

All the rest of his family can fly
But he just relaxes and eats a blackberry pie.
The next day he went to school
But he shouted I want to play pool!

When he got to school his teacher said,
'Late again, off with your head.'
Then they did a big, loud cough
What a surprise, the bird flew off!

Ritchie Vincent (8)
Glenmere Primary School

I WANT TO BE . . .

I want to be a lovely bird,
I want to be a ladybird,
I want to be a lovely cat,
I want to be a scary bat,
I want to be a lovely mum,
But I don't want to be so dumb.
I want to be a lovely finger,
I want to be a lovely singer,
I want to be a lovely ring,
I want to be a lovely king.

I seem to be reading but I am dreaming,
I seem to be trying but really I am crying.
I seem to be looking but I really am cooking.
I seem to be cracking but really I am peeking.
I seem to be picking but really I am flicking.
I seem to be leaning but really I am pulling.
I seem to be clapping but really I am tapping.
I seem to be fighting but really I am kiting.
I seem to be falling but really I am crawling.

Sajid Kadri (8)
Glenmere Primary School

GREEN POEM

What is green?
Seaweed is green
Green is the grass.

What is blue?
The sea is blue.
Blue is fresh.

What is purple?
Purple is dark
Purple is the clouds.

Hannah Barnett (8)
Glenmere Primary School

THE WHALES

The whales all go in the deep, blue sea,
All three, as deep as can be.
Deeper and deeper as fast as they can go,
Go!

Danielle Wilson (8)
Glenmere Primary School

PURPLE

Purple is quite a nice colour
Purple is quite bright,
Purple is quite nice in the day,
But you cannot quite see it at night.

Purple is quite a useful colour
It is the colour of some flowers.
We've got some purple flowers,
They're ours!

Jessica Hayes (8)
Glenmere Primary School

THE ARMY WITH THE ENEMY

Missiles blowing from the sky,
Everyone thinks they'll die!
Gunshots firing from each side,
As marshals shoot with pride.

Get into a raft and leave a time bomb
And they will have thoughts they have won.
But when it explodes
They will have . . . *dirty clothes!*

Hisham Chaudhary (8)
Glenmere Primary School

SUE

Sometimes she pretends to moo
She likes mice.
Sue is nice,
Sue is very fond of you.

Sue is very nice to you
Sue loves the shining of the sun
Sue is so much fun,
Sue is very fond of you.

Georgina Wills (8)
Glenmere Primary School

THE CHEETAH

There was a cheetah who had a lot of pace
And he was the spottiest animal around.
He even had spots on his face,
The spots were black.

He caught a deer,
It was easy
Because he had no fear
He ate it for his main meal.

He entered a race
With other animals
The cheetah didn't have to chase,
And that was the end of the race.

Lewis Prendergast (8)
Glenmere Primary School

MY POEM

I have a laugh,
My eyes are green,
I have a bath,
Then I am clean!

My age is eight,
My friend is Fay,
We opened the gate,
We had a great day!

I giggle every day,
With my friend Daisy,
We have fun when we play,
Because we're crazy!

Misha Penney (8)
Glenmere Primary School

FROST

F reezing frost, frozen trees, branches falling, people sneeze,
R ooftops covered in sparkling snow, making our noses
and fingers glow.
O ver the hills we must go, following the trail of the deep, deep snow.
S ilky snow ho, ho, ho, slippery ice not very nice.
T reading in snow everywhere you go, slushy wushy, slushy wushy,
slushy wushy,

Snow!

Daisy Dobrijevic (8)
Glenmere Primary School

GETTING A CAR

A long time ago or perhaps last week,
We went to get a car or just to take a peek
We went over the bridge that we feared,
And when we got to the building we saw a man with a beard.
We asked the man what he'd got and he replied,
'What do you want?'
'What about a Fiesta?' said Dad, but Mum answered 'Certainly not!'
But Dad had had enough of my mother and said to the man
'What's that?'
'That's a Corsa,' said the man, getting jumpy,
But Dad said 'How coarse!'
But Mum had turned a bit angry, if we didn't find a car soon,
We'd be back with our old Savanna, which had no luxury at all.
So finally we drove off with Savanna, with no new car at all
And now I can really prove that we've lost our new car and all!

Alex Carpenter (8)
Great Bowden CE School

MY FRIEND TOM NORTH

My house is a mess,
Tom North doesn't like cress.
My other friends are big and tall,
Tom is really pretty small.
Nial's dad eats orange peels,
Tom eats little meals.
Sam sat on a battered chair,
Tom has blondish hair.
My mum's car has a hooter,
Tom has a computer.
On and on playing all day
Tom will even lose the way.
Until his mum says
'Tom get your butt to bed.'

Aaron Watts (9)
Great Bowden CE School

DOG STYLE

D is for dog that everyone likes, but most people think every dog bites.
O is for Oliver a popular name, but my brother knows dogs aren't all
                                                                the same.
G is for greyhound, they run really fast, his legs are like bullets
                                                                  as they pass.
S is for Staffords, that I like best, but maybe when I'm older
                                                                I'll choose the rest.

Beth Dillon (7)
Great Bowden CE School

THE SEA

Deep blue, sparkling green,
It's the best place I have ever seen,
Seaweed here and seaweed there,
Seaweed, seaweed everywhere.

Crabs scuttle across the land,
Starfish float like they are grand,
Tiny fish swim in a pool,
The sea is so very cool.

Sand hot,
Sand cold,
Sand silver,
Sand gold.

Astrid Tooms (9)
Great Bowden CE School

SCHOOL

Girls, boys and aliens all at school
Here comes the teacher that's not a rule
Get in line before I tell
Here she is, Mrs Bell.
Mrs Bell is here
Time to work, so get in gear
'You give the maths books out
And you stop the tears.'

Lana Johnson (9)
Great Bowden CE School

AEROPLANES

Aeroplanes flying
High
    And
        Low
Across the classroom,
Against the doors,
Against the walls,
And against the teacher's head.

Flying
    High
        And
            Low
Across the desks,
Faster and faster,
It's a fantastic sight
Paper aeroplanes everywhere.

Sam Tyrell (9)
Great Bowden CE School

I HEARD IT EVERYWHERE

I heard it in the street.
I heard it in the pool.
I heard it in the playground.
I heard it in the loo.
I heard it in the bath tub.
I heard it down the lane
What did I hear?
You work it out yourself.

Hannah Brittan (8)
Great Bowden CE School

DOLPHINS

Dolphins, dolphins,
Dolphins in the sea.
The sea is very rough.
Dolphins, dolphins,
Look at me.
They click, whistle, squeak,
Back to the sea.

Amy Brewster (9)
Great Bowden CE School

THE TROUBLE WITH MY SISTER

The trouble with my sister
Is that she can't do a thing
She moans, she moans and that's the thing.
She can't stop kicking, she can't stop punching
Then she just cries
And I get the blame.

Michael McHugo (8)
Great Bowden CE School

THE SEA

We went to the sea
Dad and I,
We hired a boat
Till the evening grew nigh.
'Come on son' said Dad,
But when we left
I felt sad.

Kay Williams & William Bromley (8)
Great Bowden CE School

MY LITTLE SISTER

My little sister is a pain,
My little sister steals my toys,
My little sister drives me insane.

My little sister is in reception,
My little sister is only four,
My little sister gets me detention.

My little sister is now in year one,
My little sister does not learn,
When my little sister comes home she makes such a noise,
That your ears go ding dong.

Ruth Beacher (8)
Great Bowden CE School

PET CRAZY

Dogs, cats, fishes and frogs
I am pet crazy, nothing is wrong.

Spaniels, Dalmatians, Labradors
And not forgetting the newly born pups.

Caterpillars, butterflies, spiders and 'scorps'
They're all creepy crawlies with no doubt.

Dogs, cats, fishes and frogs
I am pet crazy, nothing is wrong.

Aled Williams (9)
Great Bowden CE School

TEACHERS, TEACHERS EVERYWHERE

Teachers, teachers they teach you a lot.
Teachers, teachers everywhere.
Teachers, teachers
They are such a pain
And my teacher's name is Jane the Pain.

Teachers, teachers
They are quite cruel.
Teachers, teachers
They are quite cool.
Teachers, teachers
They drive you up the wall.

Georgia John-Charles (8)
Great Bowden CE School

MY DOGS

Our dog Fred ate all the bread.
Our dog Dash ate all the hash.
Our dog Pete ate all the meat.
Our dog Davy ate all the gravy.
Our dog Toffee drank all the coffee.
Our dog Jake ate all the cake.
Our dog Trip ate all the dip.
And the worst, from the first -
My dog Fred pooped on my foot.

James Sands (8)
Great Bowden CE School

WAKE UP

Messy, blond, sweaty hair
Standing up in all directions.
Black-blue bags under half-open, tired eyes.
Dopey, dizzy, unidentified slouching person
Unaware of any happenings around the world.
Surroundings all blurred
Drowsy brain and wobbly legs
Staggering about while getting up
Falling over anything in the way.
Trying unsuccessfully to bring senses
Back to planet Earth.
Brain saying 'Go back to bed!'
Trying to resist
'Go back to bed!'
Arguing against my brain.
Mum shouting 'Wake up!'
Brain saying 'Go back to bed!'
This happens every morning
When I wake up.

Jonathan Millican (10)
Great Dalby Primary School

THE RIVER

The river is grand,
So strong and mighty,
It pours down the valley,
Draining the land.

It cuts through the rock,
Eroding and corroding,
Grinding and eating
Eating the lot.

It's used for farming,
Recreation and transport,
Fishing and industry,
And it's ever so calming.

But in the towns,
When it floods,
It's cleared of joy,
And people drown.

Jonathan Smith (10)
Great Dalby Primary School

SWIMMING IN THE SEA

I was swimming in the sea
Swimming in the sea,
Swimming in the sea.
Water is cold
Current is strong
Waves are giant
I was swimming in the sea.
Current is going around and around
Waves are crashing, rolling up and down
I was swimming in the sea.
Swimming, swimming
Shore's getting further away
Swimming towards the shore
Panic, panic
Swim, swim
Arms are tired,
Am I swimming
Or am I drowning, drowning?

Tiffany Hodges (10)
Great Dalby Primary School

THE CLOUDS

Floating through the morning sky
The sun gleaming through
Clouds slowly moving across the sky
Like a boat running down a stream
Flying over the frosty snow-capped mountains.

The sky darkens,
The clouds rush
Like enormous waves in the sea.
A motorway of dark grey clouds
Growing faster and faster
Thunder getting louder and louder
Like a drum.
Getting closer and closer
Then the dark heavens open
The rain pours down
Back to Earth
Then the sky becomes lighter
The sun gleams through clouds once again.

Daniel Johnston (10)
Great Dalby Primary School

BORING BILLY

My friend Billy is very, very boring,
My friend Billy is very, very boring.
If we play a game he says it's very boring,
If he reads a book he says it's very boring.
If he hears a song he says it's very boring.
But when we are doing something very, very boring
He enjoys it!

Mark Dixon (11)
Great Dalby Primary School

MILK

Milk - just yucky!
It's horrible,
It's sad.
My sister really loves it
But we're opposite - that's that.
Who cares about the calcium?
Who cares about your teeth?
It tastes just horrible
It's even worse than meat
Milk, milk.
Horrible, slimy white stuff
All poured into a glass
It's all bubbly and plain
Good thing it doesn't stain.
When it's sour
It's in a right state
Milk, milk . . . milk.

Laura Greaves (10)
Great Dalby Primary School

THE STORM

All night is quiet until
The storm starts.
Rain dropping down rapidly,
Thunder crashing,
Lightning flashing every three seconds,
Wind blowing houses down,
People running for their lives,
Animals scared stiff.
Suddenly the storm stops.

Sienna Brooks (10)
Great Dalby Primary School

SCHOOL

Schools are good,
Schools are bad,
Schools can be fun,
Schools can be powerful.

Schools on Mondays,
Schools on Tuesdays,
Schools on Wednesdays,
Thursdays and Fridays.

We write, we count
We do our times tables
Poetry too, a little English
That's what we do.

Saturdays and Sundays
We get them off
Do what we want to do
That's not so bad is it.

Schools are good,
Schools are bad,
Schools can be fun,
Schools can be powerful.

Georgia Stevens (8)
Great Dalby Primary School

JOSEPH

Joseph had a coat
Of many different colours
From his fond father.

Anton Brookes (10)
Great Dalby Primary School

SADNESS

I was upset,
I was sad.
I was crying,
I was sad.
I was tearful,
I was sad.
I was lonely,
I was sad.
I was miserable,
I was sad.
I was gloomy,
I was sad.
I was lost,
I was sad,
I was sad.

Paul Byrne (10)
Great Dalby Primary School

SPACE

10, 9, 8, 7 . . . bang
A rocket is firing like a bullet
Into space
Bright scorching
Red flames fire
Out the back
Suddenly it's gone into space.
I should imagine it's passing the planets
Mercury, Mars, the red planet
I wonder what it's like
Up there in space.

James Longden (8)
Great Dalby Primary School

RIVERS

Freezing cold waters
Creeping up through
A stretch of murky ground.
Rushing down the mountain,
Getting faster and faster
And widening.
Streams running into
The widening river.
Going down waterfalls,
Meandering, flowing past the flood plain,
Making an estuary
And going into the sea.

Adam Houghton (9)
Great Dalby Primary School

SADNESS

I'm always missing people, family and friends
When I'm enjoying myself, poof . . . they disappear.
First of all there was my dad,
Now I only see him every so often.
Then there was my best friend who left to live in Australia,
Now I only hear from her every so often.
Then there was my friend,
I've known her for six years
Now she's moved to Lincolnshire
And I only get e-mails every so often.
Then there was my hamster
Who lived a long life,
But I *don't* hear from him every so often.

Laura Baker (11)
Great Dalby Primary School

BOAT ON THE SEA

Jumping, wavy
Boats on the sea
Storms ahead, breaking wind.

Blowing from side to side
Sailing on the big ocean.
Shivery nights while sleeping.
Creaking noises
Bumping into rocks.

Sinking,
    Down,
        Down,
            Down.

Jessica Collin (9)
Great Dalby Primary School

IN MY MIND

In my mind,
The river's flowing by.
My favourite animal the dolphin,
Brain waves,
Singing sleepily,
Drifting off to dreamland,
Very sleepy,
In a trance,
Can't stop,
Too busy,
Drifting off to dreamland,
In the waves the sounds you hear,
In my mind.

Catherine Bates (9)
Great Dalby Primary School

HIDDEN LIFE

The wood, a blanket of berries and leaves
Or that's how we see it.
In the real wood
Nothing's as it seems
Deer stags
Staring at the moonlit wood
Standing tall
A shadow cast upon the world.
Birds fluttering from tree to tree
At the sight and sound of danger.
Rabbits sweet and cuddly
Some might think
But in the wild they're scuttering
For their lives.
We come to the wood itself
Trees some old, some new
In the night shapes emerge
Fog floats past. Eerie!
Scary!
You feel lost in time
And your mind goes blank.
You scream
Help! Help!
One final painful scream,
And you have fallen asleep by a tree
 . . . Or have you?

Grace Orgill (10)
Great Dalby Primary School

SHEEP

Sheep lie,
Sheep die,
Sheep eat,
Sheep bleat.

> They are cute,
> Cuddly too
> They don't eat carrots but we do.

Sheep lie,
Sheep die,
Sheet eat,
Sheep bleat.

> They could be black,
> They could be white,
> But they're better white so you can see
> Them at night.

Sheep lie,
Sheep die,
Sheep eat,
Sheep bleat.

> Sheep eat grass,
> Sheep eat hay,
> Every sheep sleeps each day.

Sheep are black,
Sheep are white
Sheep aren't good at being quiet at night.

Lucy Fraser (9)
Great Dalby Primary School

RIVERS

I can see the river
It is flowing by.
Down and down the mountain
Swerving and swifting.
The sound of the waterfall, falling
The sunset going down
The picture is in my mind.
The river is starting to meander
Getting slower and slower.
The flood plain is dry
The river is just running past.
One more turn
And it meets the sea.

Miranda Myers (9)
Great Dalby Primary School

THE COUNTRYSIDE

Through the knee-high grass,
Look up at the big, blue sky
With cotton wool-like clouds.
Look down at the active bugs
Finding fresh, cool water close by
Hear the galloping of a horse,
With his sensitive ears.
But going onto other things
The flowers make the fields glow,
Everything is smart and very beautiful
Always something to look forward to
Walking through the countryside.

Abigail Millican (8)
Great Dalby Primary School

THE RIVER

I'm swimming in the river
I've just seen an otter,
Looking for her kit
Oh no! The river's pulling me
Down and down and down,
I'm on the river bed!
A pike is hurrying past me
Looking for food
The current pulls me,
Up and up and up.
I flow down the river,
Into the estuary
Suddenly a big rush of water pulls me down
Down
    Down
        Into the sea!

I'm on the sea bed
A puffer fish swims by me
I'm pulled to the surface
Onto the beach
That's the end of my journey.

Emily Fionda (8)
Great Dalby Primary School

MY SISTER

My sister is a pain
She makes it rain
Down the drain
When she is a pain
I go insane.

My sister can be good
Likes to eat lots of pud
Plays around in the mud
Being as stupid as she could.

She doesn't like potatoes,
She doesn't like beans,
She doesn't like people wearing jeans.

Eli-Louise Lowe (10)
Great Dalby Primary School

A GAME BOY IS . . .

A Game Boy is a coloured box,
It is the thing that keeps me alive,
It is a mini computer.

A Game Boy is a digital TV
It is a portable computer,
It is the coolest thing on earth.

A Game Boy is a battery-powered toy,
It is a micro-super toy,
It is my favourite toy.

Mark Lawton (9)
Husbands Bosworth CE Primary School

A HORSE

A horse has four legs
That look somewhat like pegs,
A horse has a mane covered in grass stain,
A horse has a tail that is so tatty,
It could get caught in a nail.
A horse has two ears,
If you touch them he rears.
A horse has a back,
You sit on him to have a hack.
A horse has some eyes,
That look like stars in the skies.
A horse has a shoe made of metal,
They would melt if they went in a kettle.
A horse has a coat of fur,
In the cold it wouldn't go brrr . . .
I feel so sorry for the owner,
I'm sure that horse will never be mine!

Catherine Price (11)
Husbands Bosworth CE Primary School

THE MOON

The moon is a pie high in the sky,
It is a milk top floating in buoyant space.
It is a football paused in the sky.
It is a hot air balloon bobbing up and down.
It is a marshmallow smiling still.
It is a yo-yo hanging by its string.
It is a silver tin rolling in space.

Gray Inman-Hall (10)
Husbands Bosworth CE Primary School

WHAT IS A CLOCK?

A clock is a skeleton walking up the stairs.
It is like a horse chasing a fox down the road.
It's church bells ringing at one o'clock.
It's the tall monster staring you in the face.
The small box on the mantelpiece.
The hands are a face.
A person stood with an old fashioned moustache.
The time is ticking away.
It's gone in the click of a finger.
The seconds have gone.
The hours have gone.
Every second, minute and hour *Puff* it's gone
Never to be seen again.

Daniel Hickman (10)
Husbands Bosworth CE Primary School

COKE

It tastes quite nice,
With lots of ice.
It's black and brown,
So guzzle it down.
It's so fizzy, it makes you burp,
It's too nice for a little twerp.
It makes you shiver,
And stand straight as a quiver.
So if you want a laugh and joke,
Drink lots of yummy, yummy coke!

Joseph Day (10)
Husbands Bosworth CE Primary School

THE MYSTERIOUS BAT

Banana leaves flapping, gliding, flapping, gliding;
An evil face with beady eyes,
Stick legs disappear in flight;
Built-in computer high sensors like a stealth plane,
In the day bewildered only to fly when the moon is present;
Thrusting towards insects dividing
Then subtracting one by one;
Ears the size of the Big Apple,
Sharp spears coming out of the dreaded mouth;
A gust of wind takes it high to a church tower
Where it will die in the winter sky.
Where clutching the rough ceiling with their bony fingers;
Vigorously hanging for a day, not even shaking.

Matthew Cartmell (11)
Husbands Bosworth CE Primary School

COKE

It's really nice with
Lots of ice.
It's so fizzy,
It makes you dizzy.

It's black and brown,
So guzzle it down.
It's so fizzy, it'll make you burp.
It's too nice for little twerps.
So if you want a laugh and joke
Then drink a lot of yummy coke.

Thomas Williams (10)
Husbands Bosworth CE Primary School

WHAT IS . . . A GHOST?

A ghost is a misty shadow,
It is a ghost that lives in the attic.
It is a phantom that comes out at night.

A ghost is pale and transparent,
It is a spirit that comes back to haunt,
It is a vision that you see at night.

A ghost is a gust of wind,
That is colder than space.
It is an imaginary thing that
Gives you a fright.

Kelly Williamson (10)
Husbands Bosworth CE Primary School

GHOST

If you ever see a ghost, run, run, run!
Or it will get you.
And if you don't know what a ghost is,
Well I'll tell you!
A ghost is a funny feeling in the spine,
A ghost is a howling dog,
It's a whistle in the wind,
It's a spirit in the trees.
It's like your whole life flashing before you,
And it will take you through the valleys and
Across the midnight sky woooooh!

Jenny Begley (9)
Husbands Bosworth CE Primary School

WHAT IS A REAL GHOST?

A ghost is thin, slow floating in the wind.
It is a piece of white cloth
It is a steaming pane of glass
It is a ball of fluff.

A ghost is like a sheet of paper flying
It is white wall with no bumps.
It is a bag floating in the night's wind,
It is like a witch flying without her broom.

A ghost is gone but it will be back
A ghost is a make-believe story,
That children believe or is it really?

Stuart Wright (9)
Husbands Bosworth CE Primary School

WHAT IS AN APPLE?

An apple is a red ball
In a fruit bowl.
It is a crisp snow
On an icy day.
It is the red
Sunset at dawn.
It is a watering
Mouth ready to bite.
It is the fresh smell
Of the sea.

Sam McWilliam (10)
Husbands Bosworth CE Primary School

HORSE RIDING

The air,
Horse riding is getting swept off
The ground.
Horse riding is like on a rollercoaster.
Horse riding, horse riding, horse riding.

First place, second place, third place,
Fourth place,
High jumps
Low jumps
All jumps
Water jumps
Trotting poles
Big horses, small ponies, mares,
Foals, geldings, stallions,
All sorts of horses.
Horse riding, horse riding, horse riding.

Jessica Asher (9)
Husbands Bosworth CE Primary School

WHAT IS . . . A CLOUD?

A cloud is a fluffy ball kicked
High in the air.
It is a cuddly toy,
Dropped down Heaven's drain.

A cloud is a car made out
Of fluff instead of fibreglass,
it's a jumpy young bird
Beginning to take its first flight.

A cloud is a bed on which
The sun or moon can position in darkness,
It is a comfortable, fluffy
Pillow on which the sun or moon can lie at night.

A cloud is a warm, cosy jumper
I wear every day.
It is a pair of warm, snug
Trousers that I can pull on.

Anna Leedham (11)
Husbands Bosworth CE Primary School

WHAT IS... THE SEA?

The sea is a massive shining mirror,
It's a vast wavy swimming pool.
The sea is a big blue puddle,
It's a great enormous plain of calm water.

The sea is a vicious dog when it's seen a cat.
The sea is a place of danger,
A place of horrid deaths.

The sea is a famous summer holiday,
Where you can splash in its calm waves.
The calm sea is a new lamb frolicking in a field.

The sea is an underwater wonderland,
With amazing coral reefs.
The sea is a home for swimming animals,
For fascinating fish.

Catherine Harvey (10)
Husbands Bosworth CE Primary School

WHAT IS A GHOST? . . .

A ghost is a sheet caught by the wind.
It's a spooky feeling.
It's the sound of curtains on a windy night.
A ghost is a terrible thing that comes to haunt you.
A ghost is the most horrible thing on earth!
A ghost is as pale as a sheet of paper.
It comes out on full moon.
It is a thing that comes out of a grave.
Beware of the ghost.

Jack Oliver (9)
Husbands Bosworth CE Primary School

THE LITTLE BLACK CAT

The little black cat fell asleep on the mat,
And started to snore,
Which was such a bore.

She prowls around,
In the dead of night,
Looking for a mouse,
That tastes just right.

Early in the morning,
On her way home.
She finds a nice patch,
Of long grass and,
Goes to sleep.

Colin Mackellar (10)
North Luffenham CE Primary School

HOLIDAYS

Holidays, holidays, where shall I go?
Over the sea to see what I can see.
Holidays, holidays, where shall I go?
In an aeroplane, to see the mountain glow.

Holidays, holidays, where shall I go?
On a train through a tunnel, I just don't know.
Holidays, holidays, where shall I go?
In the car going to the fair.

Holidays, holidays, where shall I go?
Walk to the beach, I love to see hundreds and
Hundreds of people shouting yippee.
Holidays, holidays, where shall I go?
On a bus to the Island of Scilly where
The green grass will grow.

Kirsty Baines (10)
North Luffenham CE Primary School

DINOSAURS

Some are *big* and some are *small*
Some are long and some are tall.
Some walk fast some walk slow
Some can fly, sometimes low.
Some are fierce some are hopeless,
Like the gentle giant Diplodocus.
Some are herbivores some are carnivores
This is what I call dinosaurs.

John Reidy (10)
North Luffenham CE Primary School

WINTERTIME

I see icy icicles drip, drip, dripping on the floor.
I see sparkling snow drop, drop, dropping from the sky.
I see dead and blackened trees creak, creak, creaking way up high.
I see children playing near, clap, clap, clapping everywhere.
I see shining winter snow, snow, snowing on by.

Sarah Fallow (11)
North Luffenham CE Primary School

LITTLE KITTY

Outside
Behind the door
A little kitty stands
Longing for attention and love
From us.

Natasha Schofield (11)
North Luffenham CE Primary School

BMX

My BMX is all silver and new
The tyres are wide and the steering is true.
I ride like the wind when the weather is fine.
The feeling is great when I speed past the line.
Approaching the ramp at terrific light speed.
I fly of the ramp into space as I please.

Daniel Vincent (10)
North Luffenham CE Primary School

MY BEDROOM

My room is like a racetrack
My bed the main stand.
The Scalectrix is the track,
My drawer the pit stop
And the lego men the crowd.

Oscar Dejardin (10)
North Luffenham CE Primary School

A FROSTY MORNING

Frosty morning bright and cool,
Walking carefully off to school.
All the roads are sparkling white,
Everything is a beautiful sight.
Icicles frozen on a gate,
Slowly melting at a steady rate.
Trees are bare now leaves are gone,
See a squirrel hop along.

Abi Corby (10)
North Luffenham CE Primary School

IN MY BATH

In my bath just duck and me
Sailing on the foaming sea.
The bubbles are the bubbling foam
The water is the fishes home!

Klaus Osterlund (10)
North Luffenham CE Primary School

MY BEDROOM

If you walk into my bedroom
My very nasty bedroom
You'll find monsters in my bedroom
That will give quite a fright.

My bed is going to gobble you
My keyboard's going to deafen you
My door will lock you in
My curtains block the light.

When I walk in my bedroom
(Once my bed has gobbled you)
The monsters will protect me
And keep me safe all night.

Meredith Newby (10)
North Luffenham CE Primary School

MY GRANDAD

My Grandad is old
He sits in his chair,
And he has spiky,
Grey coloured hair.

He likes to read books
About Rutland and war.

He tells me long stories
But he isn't a bore.

My Grandad is simply the best.

Daniel Greetham (10)
North Luffenham CE Primary School

AUTUMN

Autumn is a great season.

Apples falling from the trees
Orange, brown, yellow and red leaves float
Through the sky.
Melting frost trickles slowly down my cheek.

Children playing joyfully with conkers
Spiders and their webs float through the cold
And breezy air.
The frost clings tightly onto each piece of grass
What a beautiful effect.

Trees getting ready for winter
New buds forming
And inside the chestnut shell it feels soft and milky.

Natalie Morrison (10)
North Luffenham CE Primary School

DAISY THE DOG

Daisy the lazy dog
Sleeps and snores all day long
She jumps on to a log
And when we get near her
She jumps on to the ground
And turns all around and
Around and gets herself dizzy
And she wants to play when
She is daft and dizzy she likes
You to stroke her when she is
Not so dizzy.

Kirsty Everton (10)
North Luffenham CE Primary School

FOOD

I like to eat pizza,
It has melted mozzarella cheese all over it.
I like the pineapples and olives and pepperoni,
The crusty bits are really nice.

I like to eat jacket potatoes,
They have a soft inside and you can put butter on them.
I like the skin on the outside, it is sometimes crispy or chewy.

I like Chinese takeway,
It just tastes so nice,
I like the sweet and sour, and the noodles.

I like Indian curries,
Especially the naan bread, it cools down the hot taste.

I like Weetabix,
I have them in the morning every day.
I can eat 48 in one week.

James Newsham (10)
North Luffenham CE Primary School

SHEEP

Sheep are silly, sheep are daft,
Sheep could just not sail a raft.

Sheep are clever, sheep are witty,
Sheep go down to New York City.

Sheep are fluffy, sheep are *there,*
But sheep say nothing but *Bbaaaarrrr.*

Chloe Thompson (10)
North Luffenham CE Primary School

IN A LAND OF DREAMS

If I had a dream it would be about . . .
A wonderful land long begone.

Where dragons roamed the earth,
Searching for bronze, silver and gold.

Wizards cast their spells,
And summoned powers known no more.

Great and mighty bears,
Fought throughout their days.

But the mighty and feared Saurun,
Ruled the earth as Dark Lord.

Sophie King (10)
North Luffenham CE Primary School

MOLLY THE MOGGY

My cat Molly is a silly old thing,
Chasing leaves is her kind of thing.
But when it comes to food,
No old tin cat food,
But salmon she cries.

My cat Molly is a silly old thing,
When bedtime comes, she climbs on in.
Come on, move over, make room for me,
And with a purr, she's asleep again.

Matthew Atkins (10)
North Luffenham CE Primary School

SEA

Sea can be quiet,
Sea can be loud,
Sea can be calm,
Sea can be rough,
Sea can be cold,
Sea can be warm.

Andrew Williams (10)
North Luffenham CE Primary School

MY TIP

Mum says it's a tip
To me it is a ship.
Mum says it is a tip
To me it is an airstrip.
Mum says it's a tip
To me it's a spaceship.
Mum still thinks it is a tip
To me it is what I want it to be
It's my room.

Matthew Turville (10)
North Luffenham CE Primary School

AT THE SEASIDE

We played in the sand and had an ice cream,
The sea was cold so it made us scream.
We made a sandcastle with our bucket and spades,
The sun came out so we played in the waves.

Mid afternoon we went to the pier,
We sent a postcard saying 'Wish you were here.'
A ride on the rollercoaster was such fun,
We got really hot from the blazing sun.

Anna Saunders (10)
North Luffenham CE Primary School

SPEECH

It works all your life
And it's always with you
You use it a lot every day
But it does not take pay
You can use it to inspire
Or mightily discourage
And you can insult in the worst way
So an important part of life it plays.

Fergal Hainey (11)
North Luffenham CE Primary School

GIRLS

Girls are girls but before that they dance
Around in dresses and pretty hats.

When they're older they are more fun
They have sleepovers with sticky buns.

They love shopping and pillow fights
Dancing around till after midnight.

Bianca Jantuah (10)
North Luffenham CE Primary School

FISHES

Fishes are my favourite things,
Swimming along with those mystical fins,
All different colours red, green and blue,
Swimming along all around you.
Some swim fast, some swim slow,
Some swim very, very low.
Some are thin and some are fat,
Some are thick and some are flat.
Then again they come and go,
All different kinds now you know.

Andrew Sampson (10)
North Luffenham CE Primary School

I AM

I am an old watering can.

Once I would hold two litres of water.
I was used every day.
I had to be filled up twice to water the whole garden.
I had red paintwork with a big daisy on my side.
The other watering cans were jealous of my paintwork.
My owner took me to all of the flower shows.

But now I am an old watering can all rusted up
With a hole in the bottom.
Some of my paintwork has been scratched off.
My owner uses a hose now.
Soon I will be used as a flower pot,
With beautiful flowers in it, hopefully.

Lewis Farrow (10)
Overdale Junior School

SEASIDE TIDE

All the wind in my hair
The sun, the sea, the salty air.
Everybody swimming in the sea.
All the waves, jump over me.
At the seaside it's nice and cool
I especially like the rock pool.
Making castles in the sand
And knocking them over with my right hand.

Aimee Noon (9)
Overdale Junior School

PARK

In the park there are romantic couples
Sat on the grass
Children run, jump, swing and slide.

Josh Smith (9)
Overdale Junior School

MY NIGHTMARE MEAL

To make my nightmare meal I'll need;
A jar full of beetles blown away in a breeze.
A couple of scabs off an elephant's knees.
An old, grey cat with plenty of fleas,
And some absolutely, positively, smelly, old cheese.
A pot of stings from some bumblebees
And a deadly shark from the deep blue seas.

Mary Goodhart (10)
Overdale Junior School

I AM...

I am an old teddy bear
Once I got to go anywhere.
I went to the swimming baths and
Swam around with my owner (pulling me along).
We went on the computer together and we played games.
I was warmly tucked up in her bed at night.
My fur shone and it was brushed every day.
I had two big, blue button eyes and a big round smile.
My stitching was extremely well done.

But now I'm locked in the closet
Sitting behind fishing rods and old dolls.
My fur is all messy,
My big eyes have gone all brown and mouldy.
My big, round smile seems to be coming down my face.

Soon I am going to the car boot sale
And I'm hoping someone likes me.
So everything can happen again
(The good things!)

Sophie Evans (10)
Overdale Junior School

AT THE BEACH

On the sandy beach
Where the seagulls glide and screech.
The seaweed sways from side to side
As starfish try to hide.
The rushing tide comes in at last
You have to leave pretty fast.

Jessica Archer (9)
Overdale Junior School

I AM...

I am an old teddy bear.

Once I went to a wonderful theme park.
I went on every ride that my owner went on.
She took me on the best ride there,
It was called 'Shockwave'.
My eyes sparkled blue,
My fur was bright and clean,
I slept in a very comfy bed every night.

But now my eyes have fallen out,
My ears are falling off,
I have pen marks all over me,
I am kept under the bed all day.

Soon I will be little bits and pieces.
All chewed up by my owner's dog!
Then my stuffing will be used to make pillows!

Hend Ainine (10)
Overdale Junior School

LOVE

Love is rosy red.
It smells like the colourful flowers
Growing in the fields.
Love has the taste of ripe strawberries
Covered in sugar.
It sounds like the wonderful, calming music.
It feels like soft velvet.
Love lives in the best place,
At the top of your heart.

Hannah Sanderson (10)
Overdale Junior School

I Am

I am an old desk.

Once I was in tip top condition,
Varnished and full of life.
I used to stand proudly in the classroom,
And think I was better than the rest.
And at breaktime I used to say to myself
'I love being a desk!'
I held pencils, pens and books.

But now I am a disgrace,
With my surface all scratched and battered.
Bumped and bruised.
I'm covered in ink and full of holes.

Soon I will be smashed, and cut up into parts.
Made into something better, I hope!

__Christopher Green   (10)__
__Overdale Junior School__

My Budgie

He's mine,
I would cry
If he should die.

He can't do a high five
But in budgie language he says 'hi!'

But I,
I wonder why?
Why did I ever call him 'Good Boy'?

__Maya Lamoudi   (10)__
__Overdale Junior School__

I AM...

I am an old sharpener.
Once I was red and orange
I was always kept safe and clean.
I was always used and never got lost.
I was always on a desk or bedside.
I was always with her (my owner).

But now all my paint is worn off and
So I am now a horrible silver and black.
I am never cleaned.
I am always lost and hardly looked for.
Soon I will be thrown away.
All broken to pieces.

Rattan Flora (10)
Overdale Junior School

I AM

I am an old chair.

Once I could smell the sweet sensation of success.
When my owner sat on me it wasn't uncomfortable.
It was pleasant, more relaxing like being on a beach.

And four year old Harry used to pretend that I was on a
Mission to blow up Mars.

But now I'm in a timber factory
Put in an area called tender wood
Myself I think it would be called tender heart.

Soon I shall be chopped up and turned into a snooker cue,
I don't mind what I am as long as it's not a chair.

Joseph Clowes (10)
Overdale Junior School

I AM

I am an old, blue squeaky dog.

Once, Susie couldn't let go of me.
I was the best thing in her life.
I was in extremely good condition.
My fur was glossy.
My blue eyes sparkled in the sun.
Susie couldn't get to sleep with
The thought of me not being by her side.
I was the best thing to her and she was to me.
I didn't know what I would do without her.

But now I am upstairs in the attic
Being squashed by other toys in a cardboard box.
I feel like I have been forgotten
Maybe, just maybe I have.

Soon I will be either chucked in the dustbin with
The smelly rubbish or given to a charity shop.
Who knows.

Nicola Davis (10)
Overdale Junior School

HAPPINESS

It's purple, blue and pink.
It smells like sweet sugar-plum flowers.
It tastes like marshmallows and sweets.
It sounds like birds singing in the morning.
It feels like being kissed by pixies.
It lives in the buds of flowers.
    It's happiness.

Jessica Sanders (9)
Overdale Junior School

I Am...

I am an old steam train.

Once I used to whiz along the tracks.
I was faster than any other train.
My coat was bright red glimmering in the sunlight.
Everyone wanted a ride on me.
My driver was a kindhearted man.
If I ever got rusty, my driver would clean me.
I thought my driver would never abandon me.
All the hills were no problem for me.
I used to go all over the UK.
I went to Scotland, Wales
But in England everyone knew me.

But now I have a driver who doesn't polish me.
Now I am not the fastest train.
If I ever get rusty my driver wouldn't clean me.
Now I am rusty.
Some hills are a problem for me.
Now hardly anyone knows me.

Soon I shall not be used at all
But I shall stay in my shed.

Ian Knibbs (10)
Overdale Junior School

At The Seaside
(Haiku)

All my scraggy hair
Blowing in the cold soft wind
Always nice and fair.

Carrieann (8)
Overdale Junior School

ANIMAL POETRY

The cat meows in the middle of the night.
It's black and white.
It's ready to bite and scratch in a fight.

The cat cuddly and furry and beautiful
It's soft and gentle
It's fast asleep with us in the house.

Leighanne Holmes (9)
Overdale Junior School

THE SEASIDE POEM

In the middle of the beach
The sandcastle lay waiting for the seaweed
To slide away.
The seagulls watch the seaweed
To slide away.
The crabs hang onto the seaweed
To slide away.

Harriet Pearson-Coe (8)
Overdale Junior School

WHITE TIGER

Tiger, tiger, its skin's all creamy.
When the sun shines its fur's all gleamy.
It sits at night on the ground,
And then hunches his back all round,
And waits to pounce on his prey,
So he's fit and full ready for next day.

Beth Edwards (8)
Overdale Junior School

SEASIDE

The sea crashing against the rocks
Sand shining in the sun
A starfish flittering brightly against the shore.
Its feet covered with the sea.
Lapping around the broken sandcastle.

Megan Hellmuth (9)
Overdale Junior School

THE MAGIC BOX

I will put in my box a spaceship
Which is as fast as the speed of light,
As hard as concrete and feeling strong.
I will put in my box an alien which is as slimy as gunge.
As fast as a car and has black eyes like space.
I will put in my box a motorbike which is flashy
As flashy as a shining mirror and flows along like the sea.

Edward Olszewski (10)
Overdale Junior School

SEASIDE

A starfish lives in the blue sparkling sea.
The seagull flies in the nice warm sky.
The sandcastle is solid as a rock.
The sand is soft as you walk on it.

Emma Moore (8)
Overdale Junior School

THE MAGIC BOX

I will put in my box;
My first puppy yelping.
And bouncing around.

I will put in my box;
The swish of my Indian dress
As I twirl around.

I will put in my box;
The glisten of my watch
Jumping and hovering.

I will put in my box;
The gleam of a cat's eye
As it eyes a small mouse.

I will put in my box;
The fluff of a white cloud
As it sails through the air smoothly.

My box is fashioned from silver with red,
Blue and green gems dotted about.
It has gold hinges and a silver lock
That goes with a silver key.
It has wishes in the corners.

Rosie Tamhne (10)
Overdale Junior School

WISH, WISH, WISH

I wish I could swim one thousand miles
I wish I had loads of computer games.
I wish I had ice cream in great piles.
I wish I had a different name.

I wish I went to live in France,
I wish I had lots of money.
I wish I had a massive lance
I wish I was really funny.

Matthew Li (8)
Overdale Junior School

HOPE

Hope is white.
Hope smells like flowers.
Hope tastes like honey.
It sounds like butterflies fluttering.
It feels like a star.
It lives by the waterfall on a flower.

Ashley Wright (9)
Overdale Junior School

WISH, WISH, WISH

I wish I had a little chick
I wish I could fly.
I wish I had a friend called Mick
I wish my friend didn't die.

I wish I had a ginger cat
I wish I had a big chocolate egg.
I wish I had a little bat
I wish I had a friend called Meg.

Alex Owczarek (8)
Overdale Junior School

THE ARMY VOYAGE

The camp starts with terrible smells.
The camp comes with starving people.
The camp continues with begging people.
The camp comes with horrible sounds.
The camp comes with picking up weapons.
The camp continues with pestering shouts.
The camp comes with scary screams.
The camp ends with going to war.

Joseph Little (9)
Overdale Junior School

I KNOW SOMEONE

I know someone who picked up a frog
And kissed it.
I know someone who ate the world in one gulp.
I know someone whose shoe does not fit.

Naomi Bell (9)
Overdale Junior School

VOYAGE ON AN AEROPLANE

The voyage comes with seat belts clicking.
The voyage comes with people moving.
The voyage comes with the plane landing.
The voyage comes with people eating.
The voyage comes with people screaming.
The voyage comes with reading.
The voyage comes with kissing.

Brooke Bradshaw (8)
Overdale Junior School

HAPPINESS

Happiness is orange
It smells like some roses.
Happiness tastes like strawberries.
It sounds like Eminem singing.
It feels warm and soft.
Happiness lives in the heart of people.

Ashley Hagan (10)
Overdale Junior School

THE VOYAGE

The voyage comes with the speakers talking.
The voyage comes with the train arriving.
The voyage comes with people waving.
The voyage comes with train doors slamming.
The voyage comes with the train departing.
The voyage comes with the train tooting.
The voyage comes with the train smoking.
The voyage comes with the train stopping.
The voyage comes with the train leaving.

Daniel Beaver (8)
Overdale Junior School

WAR

Is the reddest red.
It smells like gunpowder.
It tastes like raw steel.
It sounds like clashing metal.
It lives in the middle of every soldier's heart.

Samuel James (10)
Overdale Junior School

PAIN

Pain is black
It smells like syrup.
It tastes like Idex.
It sounds like a base drum.
It feels like a million knives going into you.
It lives in mountains.

Chetan Mistry (10)
Overdale Junior School

WISDOM

Wisdom is as bright as a rainbow in the sky.
Wisdom smells as sweet as the finest perfume smell.
Wisdom tastes like banana, chocolate, strawberry and
Vanilla put together.
Wisdom sounds like the sweetest music ever composed.
Wisdom feels like one of the fluffy clouds from above
Wisdom lives within our brains.

Seema Saujani (9)
Overdale Junior School

FEAR

Fear is black like night.
It smells damp and mouldy.
Fear tastes bitter and old.
It sounds like a gale force wind.
It feels cold and lonely.
Fear lives everywhere in deep, dark corners.

Francesca White (10)
Overdale Junior School

WAR

War it's bloody-red.
It smells like hot ash burning.
It tastes like a hundred-year-old glue stuck to your lip.
It sounds like a lion and dragon roaring.
It feels like you've been shot.
It lives in the god of Hell's heart.

Amit Gore (9)
Overdale Junior School

THE VOYAGE

The voyage comes with clouds rushing.
The voyage comes with passengers staring.
The voyage comes with people puking.
The voyage comes with the stewardess serving.
The voyage comes with people eating.
The voyage comes with the pilot talking.
The voyage ends with sudden landing.

Bharante Mistry (9)
Overdale Junior School

HOPE

Hope is blue like the sky
It smells like the morning sun.
Hope tastes like sweets and cakes.
It sounds like children laughing.
It feels like fluffy white snow.
Hope lives in the heart of you.

Erica Goodwin (10)
Overdale Junior School

I AM

I am an old teddy bear,
I was loved, cuddled, taken everywhere.
Admired by everyone, everything.
Surrounded by children,
Laughing, playing.
My eyes shone,
My fur was fluffy.
The stitching was neat and even.
No threadbare stitches.
But now I am old,
My arms and legs are coming off.
My eyes are not shiny.
Layers of dust cover me.
Soon I will be taken out,
To the dump,
And left,
To rot,
In piles
Of dirt.

Emma Sainthouse (11)
Overdale Junior School

LOVE

Love is a deep red.
It smells like roses in a garden.
It tastes like candy on a stick.
It sounds like calm music.
It feels sweet and cuddly.
Love lives deep in your heart.

Nicola Hoy (9)
Overdale Junior School

I KNOW SOMEONE

I know someone who can
Make their toes thump to a tune.

I know someone who can
Click their ankles to Craig David.

I know someone who can
Breathe funny like Rolf Harris.

I know someone who can
Make their tearduct come out
And leave it for four minutes.

I know someone who can
Touch their toes when she's lifted by her legs.

I know someone who can
Lick her nose.

I know someone who can
Shake your hand with their paw for a treat.

Leah White (9)
Overdale Junior School

HAPPINESS

Happiness is pink
It smells like lots of lovely flowers.
Happiness tastes like lots of ripe vegetables.
It sounds like a lovely time.
It feels soft and silky.
Happiness lives in your heart.

Stephanie Hinshaw (10)
Overdale Junior School

WISH, WISH, WISH!

I wish I had brown hair.
I wish I wasn't so fat.
I wish I owned my own fair.
I wish I had a lady cat.

I wish I didn't have to die.
I wish I knew how to dance.
I wish I knew how to fly.
I wish I never learnt to prance.

I wish life would never end.
I wish I could never be sick.
I wish I had some friends.
I wish I had a magic stick.

I wish I was twelve,
I wish I liked fish.
I wish I had an elf.
I wish, I wish, I wish.

Rebecca Smith (9)
Overdale Junior School

LOVE

Love is the colour of the sun.
It smells like blushing strawberries.
Love tastes like sweet passion.
It sounds like a highest note on a piano.
It feels like an inside of a loving heart.
Love lives in the most peaceful place in the sky.

Radhika Pabari (10)
Overdale Junior School

WISH, WISH, WISH

I wish I could dance.
I wish I could fly.
I wish I had a hound which could pounce.
I wish I was a butterfly.

I wish I had a limo
I wish I won the lottery.
I wish my dad didn't go.
I wish I made poetry.

I wish I didn't have to go to school,
I wish I could say goodbye.
I wish I had a swimming pool,
I wish I had a lullaby.

I wish I could stay up late.
I wish I could do what I want to do.
I wish you were my mate,
I wish I could be you.

Mary James (8)
Overdale Junior School

HAPPINESS

Happiness is pink.
It smells like nice summer flowers.
Happiness tastes like sweets.
It sounds like children playing and laughing.
It feels like joy.
Happiness lives in a heart of a person.

Trish Munangi (10)
Overdale Junior School

WHEELCHAIR RACE

Look, look it's the wheelchair race,
Reception to Ward 3
What a pace,
Wheelchairs whizzing all over the place.
Bang! Bang!
Bash! Bash!
One's slowing down
Give it a push.
Black, in front,
Grey's behind.
White's got stuck, never mind.
Black's going to win,
I bet you my dollar
Black's going to win oh! no!
Grey's the winner.

Baljinder Sadhra (10)
Overdale Junior School

WISH, WISH, WISH

I wish I could have deep blue eyes.
I wish I could stay up late.
I wish I had a mum that was a detective in disguise.
I wish I had another mate.

I wish I had long blonde hair.
I wish I could see my favourite pop band.
I wish I could be President Mane.
I wish I had a back garden made of sinking sand.

Ruby Cross (8)
Overdale Junior School

I Know Someone Who Can

I know someone who can,
Make their fingers a right angle and put it straight again.

I know someone who can,
Swing one arm either way and switch arms
And keep going.

I know someone who can,
Write with both hands.

I know someone who can,
Take a mouthful of water and blow it out
Of their nose.

I know someone who can,
Juggle with their eyes closed.

Richard Wale (8)
Overdale Junior School

The Train Journey

At quarter past ten the journey starts with stepping on.
The journey comes with blowing the whistle.
The journey comes with whizzing past the countryside.
The journey comes with eating crisps.
The journey comes with peeping at the town.
The journey comes with slowing down.
The journey comes with stepping off.
The journey comes with
    The end.

Rehana Dyson (9)
Overdale Junior School

BEAUTY

Beauty is fading lilac,
Beauty smells of winter jasmine.
Beauty tastes like honey.
It sounds like harmonised singing.
It feels cuddly and fluffy.
Beauty lives in the fingertips of God.

Meera Vithlani (10)
Overdale Junior School

JOY

Joy is the colour of peachy orange.
Joy smells of perfume.
Joy tastes of beautiful chocolate.
Joy sounds like calm music.
Joy feels like happiness.
Joy lives in you.

Ayisha Mistry (9)
Overdale Junior School

PEACE!

Peace is the colour of a violet bluebell
Peace smells like fresh air.
Peace tastes like sweet honey,
Peace sounds like birds singing.
Peace feels like sharing all your moments.
Peace lives in a loving heart.

Amanpreet Kaur Raja (9)
Overdale Junior School

I KNOW SOMEONE

I know someone who can jump very high and catch a fly.
I know someone who can do a run backwards.
I know someone who can balance standing on a ball for
Ten minutes without practising.
I know someone who can lift up 50kg of gold.
I know someone who can bend their toes.

Kenneth Lamb (8)
Overdale Junior School

THE AEROPLANE JOURNEY

The journey comes with ears popping.
The journey comes with sweets sucking.
The journey comes with lots of turning.
The journey comes with crashed landing.
The journey comes with slow stopping.

Davey Martin-Hanley (9)
Overdale Junior School

THE VOYAGE

The voyage comes with a train deafening.
The voyage comes with a station waving.
The voyage comes with a train packing.
The voyage comes with the wind blowing.
The voyage comes with rain dashing.
The voyage comes with the train standing.

Meera Gajjar (8)
Overdale Junior School

MY MAGIC BOX

I will put in my box;
The gulp of a goldfish,
The growl of a tiger,
The tick of a clock.

I will put in my box;
The toot of a flute,
The shine of a gem,
The tweet of a bird.

I will put in my box;
The flash of lightning,
The bang of thunder,
The clanging of keys.

I will put in my box;
The scent of a flower,
The pattern on a snowflake,
The face of my best friend.

I will put in my box;
The stickiness of a glue stick,
The hardness of a test,
The miaow of a cat.

My box is made of;
Bubbles and foam
On the corners
Are cotton wool, so if it gets a hole
Nothing will fall out.

Gemma Collins (10)
Overdale Junior School

THE MAGIC BOX

I will put in my box;
A golden fire berry from the valleys of the sun,
And a handful of milk-white dust from the moon.

I will put in my box;
A peep of a summer morning in July
And a wisp of the cold December night.

I will put in my box;
A loud *'Tong'* from the bells of Big Ben.
And a squeak of a tiny dormouse.

I will put in my box;
A thousand galloping horses,
And a few slow tortoises.

I will put in my box;
A flame of fire from the Antarctic
And an icicle from India.

I will put in my box;
A gleam of my best friend's eyes
And a flash of lightning.

I will put in my box;
A scent of a rose
And a sting of a bumblebee.

My box is fashioned from gold, silver and bronze
With fireworks on the lid and promises in the corners.
Its hinges are horse teeth from the first horse alive.

I shall ride in my box,
Galloping across the hills of Wales
Then halt in front of the river
The colour of the sky.

Cherith Johnston (10)
Overdale Junior School

WISH, WISH, WISH

I wish I could go back in time,
I wish I had a grey and white rat.
I wish I could absail and climb.
I wish I could keep a bat.

I wish I was a bunny,
I wish I could fly.
I wish I was funny.
I wish I lived in the sky.

I wish I was a famous artist.
I wish I was perfect.
I wish I dressed the smartest.
I wish I was a pet.

Alice Lathbury (9)
Overdale Junior School

WISH, WISH, WISH

I wish I had deep blue eyes,
I wish I had a horse.
I wish my friends didn't tell lies.
I wish I had a new house.
I wish my brother was nice
I wish I could see my favourite band.
I wish I had a pet mouse.
I wish I could spend a day in the sand.
I wish I had a hound.
I wish I could fly to Never-Never Land.
I wish I had a million pounds.

Lucy Smith (8)
Overdale Junior School

I KNOW SOMEONE

I know someone who can pull her thumb off
And put it on again.

I know someone who can suck her thumb
Without sucking it.

I know someone who can hold his nose
And turn red by blowing.

I know someone who can jump two metres
In the air.

I know someone who can do twenty-five rollovers
In the water.

I know someone who can do two backflips
On a trampoline and that someone is me.

Michael Lanni (9)
Overdale Junior School

THE JOURNEY ON THE ENGINE

The voyage comes with a noisy engine.
The voyage comes with a noisy rev.
The voyage comes with two wheels spinning.
The voyage comes with a helmet vibrating.
The voyage comes with leather clothes and gloves.
The voyage comes with a small window.
The voyage comes with a really fast motor.
The voyage comes without a roof.
The voyage comes with handlebars turning.
The voyage comes with an exhaust pipe steaming.

Asad Ahmed (9)
Overdale Junior School

SPARKLE, TWINKLE, FLICKER, FLASH

The sea sparkles when the sun is out.
My eyes sparkle when I'm happy.

Sparkle, twinkle, flicker, flash.

Seashells sparkle on the seashore.
Christmas decorations twinkle in my eye.

Sparkle, twinkle, flicker, flash,
Sparkle, twinkle, flicker, flash.

Diamonds flicker, flicker, flicker.

Sparkle, twinkle, flicker, flash,
Sparkle, twinkle, flicker, flash.

Naomi Tugeman (9)
Overdale Junior School

THE JOURNEY!

The voyage comes with engines muttering.
The voyage comes with wheels screeching.
The voyage comes with air freshening.
The voyage comes with ears ringing.
The voyage comes with me vomiting.
The voyage comes with family waving.
The voyage comes with children laughing.
The voyage comes with sandcastles building.
The voyage comes with the sun shining.
The voyage comes with the sky darkening.
The voyage comes with me snoring.

Sebastian Owezarek (8)
Overdale Junior School

WISH, WISH, WISH

I wish I had ten minutes a day.
I wish I had short hair.
I wish that I was born in May.
I wish I had a cuddly bear.

I wish I had short red hair.
I wish I had blue eyes.
I wish I'd never fall off a chair.
I wish I had big apple pies.

I wish I had straight hair.
I wish I was really rich.
I wish I'd never done that dare.
I wish I was on a football pitch.

Sean Womersley (9)
Overdale Junior School

ON THE VOYAGE

On the voyage a storm has appeared.
On the voyage starts the startling thundering.
On the voyage I start to tremble.
On the voyage in the kitchen, I hear crackling.
On the voyage we are waiting.
On the voyage we start munching.
On the voyage everyone starts settling.
On the voyage everyone starts standing.
On the voyage everyone starts pushing.
On the voyage everyone gets off.
And that's the end of the voyage.

Amritpal Pooni (9)
Overdale Junior School

BOAT JOURNEY

The voyage comes with noisy horns deafening.
The voyage comes with planks wobbling.
The voyage comes with waves splashing.
The voyage comes with rain splattering.
The voyage comes with plates crashing.
The voyage comes with people arriving.
The voyage comes with boats crashing.
The voyage comes with people running.
The voyage comes with people crying.
The voyage comes with people falling.
The voyage comes with things crashing.
The voyage comes with boats drowning.
The voyage comes with the sun shining.

Chandni Thakrar (9)
Overdale Junior School

VOYAGES

Voyages come with breakfast burning.
Voyages come with stomachs churning.

Voyages come with wind blowing,
Voyages come with crows crowing.

Voyages come with mice creeping,
Voyages come with quiet sleeping.

Voyages come with sticks cracking.
Voyages come with people packing.

Voyages come with silent reading,
Voyages come with humans feeding.

Renate McKenzie-Onah (8)
Overdale Junior School

THE BOAT VOYAGE

The voyage comes with boats crashing.
The voyage comes with thunder flashing.
The voyage comes with horns clattering.
The voyage comes with water splashing.
The voyage comes with the sun setting.

Brendon Jones (8)
Overdale Junior School

THE VOYAGE ON AN AEROPLANE

The voyage comes with people moving.
The voyage comes with people eating.
The voyage comes with seat belts clicking.
The voyage comes with the plane landing.
The voyage comes with people screaming.
The voyage comes with people reading.
The voyage comes with people kissing.
The voyage comes with people playing.

Christina Meadows (8)
Overdale Junior School

BATTLESHIPS

The battle comes with sergeants saluting.
The battle comes with ships-a-hooting.
The battle comes with navy blue clothing.
The battle comes with battleships firing.
The battle comes with ships-a-sinking.

Joseph Robinson (8)
Overdale Junior School

THE VOYAGE

The voyage comes with the rocket blasting.
The voyage comes with stars twinkling.
The voyage comes with people floating.
The voyage comes with the moon shining.
The voyage comes with the sun burning.
The voyage comes with orangey red planets.

Manvir Rai (8)
Overdale Junior School

MEMORY

I was tidying up today,
And I found a very old letter
Stained with tears when Lulu left.
Here take a look.

> Dear Mother,
> I am unhappy here
> For my brother gets all the attention.
> So I have come to my senses
> And have decided to leave.
> I hope I will be lucky where I'm going.
> Although I have nowhere to go.
> I'm sorry I've left you heartbroken.
>   Love
>   Lulu.

That was the letter she wrote to me,
And still has not come back.
Memories are horrible and can bring tears.

I wonder where she is?

Charlotte Clifford (10)
Ridgeway Primary School

MYSTERIES . . .

I can't see you,
I can hear you
I don't know you
Who are you?

I can't see you
I can feel you
Where are you?
Who are you?

What's happening?
I'm in the sky
Floating around
Where am I?

I must be dead
How can that be?
Maybe it was him?
Who is he?

Mysteerrriueeee . . .

Sam Robson (9)
Ridgeway Primary School

EXCITED POEM!

Excited is a rainbow,
It tastes like mint ice cream with natural beer.
Excited looks like a roller coaster going round and round,
It sounds like a firework is going to explode.
Excited is like you're on top of the universe!

Nadine Panter (10)
Ridgeway Primary School

BEFORE MY GYMNASTIC SOLO!

Called my name
Call me!
Up on stage
Tell me!
Forearm balance
Wobbling!
Full room
Frightening!
As I stand
Under the spotlight
Brightening up the room!
So may I get good marks
I say to myself
As I stand here trembling!
People cheering
Hear them!
Beating heart
Feel it!
Beautiful smile
Laugh at me!
Please!
Tell me that it's over.

Jessica Bale (10)
Ridgeway Primary School

ON MY HOLIDAY

On my holidays I like to see
The light blue sea.
On my holidays I like to see
The silver sand and pretty shells.

On my holidays I like to
Play on the beach.
On my holidays I like to
Pick up lots of shells.

Nadine Weston (9)
Ridgeway Primary School

THE RUGBY PLAYER

Rough and mean,
Sweat and blood.
Oh no! I'll never be clean,
Raging bulls driving through the mud.

It was a fun day at the ground,
My heart was going pound, pound, pound.
When I took the conversion there wasn't a sound,
After that I got tackled to the ground.

The final minutes of the game,
If we lose I'll get the blame.
If I get the scrum right,
We're gonna have a big party tonight.

I hear the final whistle go,
The heat of my body begins to flow.
I was glad that was the end of the game,
Luke Bishop . . . that's my name.

Because it was a fun day,
My manager picked me to play.
My sister wanted to buy a toy horse,
Who's the rugby player . . . me of course.

Luke Bishop (10)
Ridgeway Primary School

THE MAGIC BOX

I will put in my magic box
    A lock of green hair and a bowl of pink sea,
    A fish that flies as fast as a plane,
    A bird that swims gracefully.
I will put in my magic box
    A dancing, diving, baby bottlenose dolphin,
    Some creamy golden, Cadbury's chocolate,
    A crunchy, crinkle tooth of a crocodile.
I will put in my magic box
    A popstar that cannot sing,
    An actress that cannot act,
    And a blacky, brownish beetle from the Bahamas.

Katherine Berridge (9)
Ridgeway Primary School

THE HOWL OF THE WIND

One winter's night the sparkly,
Snowflakes floating down onto the ground like a butterfly.
The torrent river spinning like a spiral in the sky.
Icy trees whistling, and sparkling in the moonlight.

Fluffy snow, swaying in my face like someone was controlling it.
Prickly bushes pulling me in like a black hole in deep space.
Hazardous ice cracking when I ran over it.
Dark clouds peering over the sky like a tornado.
Prickly frost making me cold and quiver.
Sparkly twigs lying still on the ground,
Frozen like ice.

Ryan Reed (9)
Ridgeway Primary School

BEFORE THE MARATHON

Shouting crowd,
Cheer me.
Blowing wind,
Push me.
Cooling water,
Calm me.
Clapping hands,
Help me.
As I beat the others
In the race,
And get shattered
By the sun,
And cooled by the wind
So may I win the race,
In such fast pace,
Lead me to my victory.

Anand Patel (10)
Ridgeway Primary School

TEN THINGS IN A TEACHER'S POCKET

A set of car keys that always rattle when she moves.
A pencil as small as a fingertip.
A rubber that rubs dirty marks.
A blunt pen which doesn't work at all.
A mobile phone that rings every five minutes.
A tissue that's full of snot.
A ruler which doesn't write in a straight line,
A notepad which is full of her boyfriends' phone numbers.
A small bag full of dead ants,
A pencil case full of holes.

Liam Eyres (9)
Ridgeway Primary School

A Journey To Outer Space

We're going to outer space,
In ten seconds flat.
The boosters have fired,
That's that.

First of all we're going to Mercury,
Then we're going to Pluto.
Last of all we're going to Mars,
Then we're going back home.

When we landed on Mercury,
And explored on our space buggy,
We met a little alien,
We also met his mummy.

When we got to Pluto,
My tummy started to rumble,
Then we found there was nothing there,
Everyone started to grumble.

When we landed on Mars,
We decided to eat.
We listened to the radio,
To a band called 'Blue Beat'.

We're going home,
In ten seconds flat.
The boosters have stopped,
That's that.

Christopher Liu (10)
Ridgeway Primary School

THE FARMER GANG

First of all there's Farmer Bob,
Who likes to chase the chickens.
Secondly there's Farmer Rine,
He wears a pair of mittens.

We're the farmer gang, OK?
We're hardworking or so we say.

Next there is Farmer Ross,
Who looks after the sheep.
Don't forget Farmer Duncan,
He rides around in a jeep.

We're the farmer gang, OK?
We're hardworking or so we say.

Farmer Chris,
He's the man.
And Farmer Luke's
A football fan.

We're the farmer gang, OK?
We're hardworking or so we say.

Last of all,
There is me.
I'm Farmer Karl,
Yippeeeee!

We're the farmer gang, OK?
We're hardworking or so we say.

Kyle Lomer (9)
Ridgeway Primary School

MUMMIES

Living underneath the ground,
Waiting for treasure to be found.
Bandages unwrapping on the floor,
Walking towards the carved stone door.

Up the stairs and round the corner,
Look straight up and see the border.
Through the secret walk of doom,
Into the special treasure room.

It curses people who come in the tomb,
Of the famous Tutankhamen.
As quiet as a rattlesnake
It slithers through the dark,
You can hear a thousand miles away
The screaming of a lark.

Up more stairs and down more cellars
And into a case the mummy sleeps!

Joseph Jeacock (9)
Ridgeway Primary School

CATS AND DOGS

Cats chase dogs, dogs chase cats,
Don't forget they all chase rats.
Cats go woof, dogs go meow,
But they both like to howl.

There are cats that bark at night,
And dogs that like to hiss and bite.
There are cats that have leads,
And dogs that slip around quite free.

Charlie is my cat's name,
Chasing wool is his game.
My Nan's dog's name is Rosie,
And her basket's nice and cosy.

Rosie takes a couple of laps,
Then likes to take an hour's nap.
When Charlie has finished his game,
He likes to go to sleep again.

Ryan March (9)
Ridgeway Primary School

A CHOCOLATE MILKSHAKE

It stirs around as a light creamy brown,
It's got a soft and powdery mixture.
It's smooth.
It's good.
With grated chocolate on the top,
Which is falling in like boulders rolling down a hill.
It's creamy,
It's soft.
It smells like a chocolate sea,
That clashes and bashes at the cliff.
It's powdery,
It's bubbly,
As I stir it, the milkshake turns into a whirlpool.
It's frothy,
It's swirly,
It stirs and whines and tings as the spoon hits the glass.
It's sweet,
It's fantastic.

Christopher Partridge (9)
Ridgeway Primary School

THE BEAST OF LEGEND

This truly is a legendary beast
With a body of gold,
And wings of steel
Made to survive the cold.

He has no fear of anyone
With his fiery breath of flames,
And claws as sharp as blades.
Anyone who goes against this beast
Will surely have to pay.

He flies at night,
Searching for his prey.
With his beady eyes,
And spiky scales of a warm red colour,
He never fails.

He lives in a cave,
In the depths of the mountain,
Or maybe just in your imagination!

Alexandra Woodford (9)
Ridgeway Primary School

THE VISIBLE BEAST

With legs as long as the river Nile,
Great big teeth and a deadly smile,
With skin as tough as old shoe leather,
He moves around as soft as a feather.

He smells so bad, I think of a dump,
His awful smell it comes from his hump.
He makes the flowers droop as well,
I really hate that awful smell.

You never know if he will scratch,
And leave you with a big red patch.
Every day he stomps around,
And it makes your heart go pound.
I really do like him the least,
That ugly smelly Visible Beast!

Emma Ritchie (9)
Ridgeway Primary School

FOOD

Cheeseburger, chickenburger,
Chocolate chips!
Cakes, marshmallows
And cherry lips!

All this food I love to eat,
Really yummy for a treat!

Gooseberries are juicy,
And covered with hairs!
I love Brussel sprouts,
And adore pears!

All this food I love to munch,
Really yummy for my lunch!

I love to eat hot dogs,
Topped with onion rings.
Tomato sauce is gorgeous
I like almost anything.

All this food I love to chew,
Really yummy and tasty too!

Caroline Clayton-Drabble (10)
Ridgeway Primary School

SPOOKED!

Beware of the spooky troll.
That patiently lies in wait.
To drag you to his spine-chilling hole.
To put you on his bony dinner plate.
His blood is blue and boiling hot.
He moans ungrateful groans.
He'll boil you in his dinner pot.
Your skin, your flesh, your bones.
He'll clutch your arms and snatch your legs,
And squash you to a pulp.
He'll swallow you like a big gorilla,
Crunch, munch, gulp!
Be careful when next you go on a little walk.
Otherwise you might end up below on the troll's fork.

Chloe Reynolds (10)
Ridgeway Primary School

ME

Sometimes I am really good
Doing everything that I should.
But sometimes I am really bad,
That makes my family sad.

If I'm feeling rather down,
I cheer myself up and go down the town.
I clap my hands and stamp my feet,
And walk up and down the street.

Then I am feeling glad,
That I'm still not feeling sad.

Natalie Windle (9)
Ridgeway Primary School

YANKS AND SLAPS

Nine o'clock strikes
There's a rising roar,
The doors burst open,
The kids get crushed.

There's a spinning tornado
A punch and a shove.
A giant snore from Heaven above
And two lovebirds kissing under the table.

Big musky coats
And mousie gloves.
Boat-like trainers,
And flying doves.

Kids squashed
Cloakrooms a blast of leaves,
A crunch of break,
Kids left at stake.

A squeal and a scream,
A yank and a slap
A fat lady teacher
And a screwed up cap.

Yelling teachers
'A' bomb-like cries,
Children running
A school full of lies.

Bulky bullies,
Running away
Some kids are on holiday,
Kids are throwing paint all day.

Lewis Dyke (9)
Ridgeway Primary School

FAIRYTASTIC TALES

Cinderboy how mucky you are but,
Cinderella how much cleaner you are.
Rapunzel how much hair do you have?
Shampozel Shampozel let down your hair.
Three little pigs, three of you
Goldilocks and the three bears . . . bears.

Billy Blast oh how ugly you are,
Beauty and the Beast how romantic you are.
The big turnip how big?
The rather small turnip as small as a carrot.
The Emperor's new clothes how beautiful,
The Emperor's underwear charming.
Little Red Riding Hood you're a wolf not a girl
How about the big bad wolf?
What big teeth you have,
All the better to eat you with.

Yum Yum Yum!

Hannah Twynham (9)
Ridgeway Primary School

THE WITCH

She really was an old witch,
Her wig was grey and hairy.
She really was a bold witch,
But she wasn't really scary.

She really had a long nose,
It looked like a twig.
But everybody knows,
It didn't go with her wig.

She really was a smelly witch,
As if she were a bog.
Her friends call her Nelly Witch,
Named after her pongy dog.

Georgia Lewis (10)
Ridgeway Primary School

SADNESS

My world is black
I carry darkness
Like bricks in a sack
I live in a world of sadness.

Why do you laugh
When I am forced to cry?
Why do you enjoy life
When my people die?

Why do you smile
When I have to frown?
Why do you swim to victory
When I drown?

Why do you have fun
When I am struck with pain?
Why do you play in the sun
When I am stuck in rain?

My world is black
I carry darkness
Like bricks in a sack
I live in a world of sadness.

Liam Godlington (9)
Ridgeway Primary School

THAT SPECIAL NIGHT

As the fireworks crackle and fizz
People watch in amazement
As the fireworks blast and zoom
People watch in amazement.

As the bonfire burns
People watch in amazement.
As the bonfire crackles
People watch in amazement.

As the bonfire is lit
People watch in amazement
As the bonfire roars
People watch in amazement.

As the fireworks start blasting
People watch in amazement
As the fireworks boom
People watch in amazement.

As the bonfire stops
People look disappointed,
As the fireworks stop
People look disappointed.

Daniel Plant (9)
Ridgeway Primary School

THE WITCH'S KITCHEN

Green smelly toad skins lying on the floor
As the bubbly cauldron spits flames.

Fat black rats scuttling round and round.
Children skating on slime.

Yellow spiders creeping over the window.
The witch spins in her cape round and round.

Rolling eyeballs on a stick,
Near to some bread, ready for supper.

Brady Marlow
Ridgeway Primary School

I WISH I HAD

I wish I had a guinea pig,
It would make a smashing pet,
Or maybe I can get one from the pet shop,
Maybe from the vet.

I'd keep it in a box,
Or maybe in a cage,
Or perhaps in a dustbin,
Where he'd get in a rage.

I'd take it to my classroom
Or maybe to the park.
When it's our teatime,
We would walk in the dark.

A guinea pig is very brave
I can teach it how to swim
And to jump off a wall,
I can teach it how to play ball.

But I only have a cat,
It can't balance a ball,
Or even swim,
And my cat isn't small.

Gemma Smeeton (9)
Ridgeway Primary School

BEFORE THE RUGBY MATCH

Falling rain
Drench me,
Dancing grass
Tickle me,
Gilbert ball
Come to me,
Martin Johnson
Help me,
Kick the ball
Accurately,
Catch the ball,
Quickly,
Tackle them
Hardly,
Hear the whistle,
Finally.
Match is over
Eventually!

Matthew Gilbert (9)
Ridgeway Primary School

THE DRAGON

The dragon lives in a cave,
In a dark, damp, tiny cave.
All alone without his family,
He has no friends at all.

He breathes red hot burning fire,
And he smells like a dustbin.
He's massive and scary,
He is multi coloured too.

How he fits in that tiny cave,
Nobody knows how he does it.
It's just incredible,
They think it's impossible too.

He has great big wings,
And razor-sharp teeth.
He has huge toenails,
And giant glowing eyes.

Adam Rippin (10)
Ridgeway Primary School

SPIDER IN MY ROOM

There's a spider in my room!
He's so noisy, he is always going boom, boom, boom.
He's bright, bright green,
And very large and mean!
His eyes are an evil yellow,
You can't hear above him unless you bellow!
He might not be very hairy,
But he's still very, very scary.
He's ever so smelly,
Even more smelly than a very old welly.
He makes the world go horribly black,
It's like being put in an dark backpack!
He's over 100 feet tall!
He'll never be shown small.
He can even beat up a lion,
His howl's so loud, it sounds like a siren!
He's got horrid yellow teeth,
He steals everything, he's just like a thief!

Charlotte Allen (9)
Ridgeway Primary School

THE ALIEN SPACECRAFT

Beepers, beeping as if they were going to explode
Into one thousand pieces.
Alien pets jumping from the wall over your head,
And under your legs.
The space TV fuzzing and buzzing like a
screw stuck in an explosive device.
Aliens bouncing from the roof to the floor
Floating in the air.
Space books standing in a pile waiting
Just waiting for someone to look at
Its tatty covers or read their torn pages.
In the rooms you could smell a rosy sort
Of smell and you could taste a sweet and sour taste.
Worst of all you could hear
Screeching and screaming.
Suddenly
There was a puff of smoke
And everyone and thing went
Silent.

Emily Beaulieu (9)
Ridgeway Primary School

WINTER

It's wintertime
The bells are starting to chime.

The snow is cold
But not too bold.

The snow is nice
So is the ice.

The snow flies low
It gets on my toe.

I like the ice
But not the mice.

It's definitely not hot
There's not even a hot spot.

Samantha Fulks (9)
Ridgeway Primary School

BITE AND FIGHT

Butterflies flutter,
Bugs scutter.

Horses clop,
Kangaroos hop.

Dolphins sing,
Rabbits spring.

Lions roar,
Tigers snore.

Bears bite,
Foxes fight.

Dogs lick,
Donkeys kick.

Leopards hurry,
Ants scurry.

But I worry!

Charlotte King (8)
Ridgeway Primary School

IN A BRIGHT, BRIGHT CLASSROOM THERE WAS...

Some karma for stress,
A coat for outside if it is cold,
A tape recorder to record the children
If they were naughty,
A pot of hairspray to fix her hair,
Some chalks to write on the board,
A pack of tissues to blow her nose,
Some paracetamols for her headache,
Some sweets for good children,
A pot of pens and pencils to mark work,
Some keys as big as church keys,
A book for reading to the children,
An Alsatian to chase away nasty children,
Some make-up to look beautiful,
And a spare pencil case.

Laura Moore (9)
Ridgeway Primary School

FUTURE

The future is a rainbow,
Rosy apples on a tree,
The Simpsons' is on every day,
But only once a week in May.
Your mum becomes cruel,
But you still stay cool,
School is only one hour,
Your house becomes a tower.
So now you know what it's really like,
In the cool new brill wicked future.

Jessica Wells (9)
Ridgeway Primary School

MY PET

My pet is fluffy
My pet is poochy
My pet is a bundler,
And my pet is a fat thing.
My pet has got green eyes
But my rabbit nibbles at night.
My pet eats everything
He would eat a mouldy apple.
If you put it in his hutch
It will be gone in five minutes,
But he will nibble your fingers off.
I get him out of his hutch and let him run
Round and round the garden.

Chloe Martin (8)
Ridgeway Primary School

VIKINGS

I praise this king in his own land,
I gladly sing of his just hand.
A hand so free with golden gains,
But strongly he can rule his Danes.

To praise this lord, my broken lip ached.
A male slave would build walls,
Cover the field with manure,
Herd pigs and goats,
Dig peat (A sort of turf burned for fuel).
A female sale would grind corn by hand,
And milk cows and goats.

Sophie Barnett (8)
Ridgeway Primary School

GROWL AND HOWL

Dogs growl
Wolves howl

Rabbits bounce
Tigers pounce

Kangaroos hop
Horses clop.

Guinea pigs nibble
Dogs dribble.

Leopards leap
Rats creep.

Birds dance
Lions prance.

Pigs grunt
Lions hunt.

Flies lie,
But I cry.

Natasha Hepworth (9)
Ridgeway Primary School

I WISH I HAD AN ELEPHANT

I wish I had an elephant,
It would be an amazing pet.
I'd steal it from the circus,
With my jumbo jet.

I'd keep it in my wardrobe,
But it might scare my mum,
Because it might eat a biscuit
Or drop a crumb.

It runs around and never stops,
An elephant is a mad creature,
I'd love my own elephant,
And I'd take it to show my teacher.

But I only have a poodle,
He isn't big at all,
He just sits around,
And stares at the wall.

Hannah Kilby (9)
Ridgeway Primary School

A DREADFUL DAY BACK

I went back after I'd been on holiday and I knew
It was going to be a dreadful day.

When I was called even my nickname sounded new.

I didn't answer
I was thinking of a dog named Rancer.

Everyone learned more than me
Even Qweneth Hanky who's worse than me.

Everyone ate their dinner
Except me because I grazed my knee.

I was late for dinner
My teacher said I was a great grinner.

At the end of the school day
Someone pushed me out of the way.
I don't think it was a great day.

Dominic Reed (9)
Ridgeway Primary School

NEW DOG

I've got a new golden retriever
She is so-ooadorable.
Dad says she is rather nice and rather pretty!
She is quite beautiful!
I think she is definitely suitable.

She stares at me with wondering eyes
As she sniffs with her cold wet nose.
The tasty smells of Cornish pies
She barks loudly at me
With her wagging tail
She is friends with me you see.

I like the way she licks my hand
As I come through the door.
She chews Dad's slippers
That are on the carpeted floor.
Her perfect paws are all so soft
She likes to sleep in our cold loft.
She's mine!
She's Mine!

Kirstie Melville (8)
Ridgeway Primary School

MY SISTER

I have a sister
She is five years old.
She talks a lot . . .
My sister and my mum are bossy.
My sister's name is Polly.
I love her.

Edward Crowe (9)
Ridgeway Primary School

MR MOSS THE BOSS

Mr Moss is our boss.

He cleans the loos
With all the poos.

He grooves
As he hoovers.

He hops,
As he mops.

He eats
As he sweeps.

He winks,
As he cleans the sinks.

He preaches
At the teachers.

He puts in light bulbs
Whilst he kicks balls.

He calls people trouble,
When they're in a muddle.

He opens doors,
As he cleans the floors.

He's a coach of many sports,
Like tennis with tennis courts.

I'll tell you a secret about Mr Moss,
He thinks he's boss but don't tell Mrs Fox!

Alice Learey (9)
Ridgeway Primary School

THE ALIENS UFO

In the dark and gloomy UFO, red emergency buttons glinted
In the dim light of the strange spacecraft.

Large fiddly knobs were going round and round
All by themselves, gave me the creeps.

Wide passageways that went on forever led to every room.

There was spooky music wherever you went,
You just couldn't get away from it.

Some doors were jammed,
They were probably secret places
Where they operated on human brains.

It had a smell of alien slime, and they must have a dog somewhere,
Because I could smell its poo.

But most importantly of all the green and yellow
                Aliens!

Toby Burbidge (8)
Ridgeway Primary School

I LOOKED UPON A STAR

I looked up at the stars,
And they dazzled in the sky.
I saw someone looking at them from Mars,
And he was looking at me. . .

I wish I could drive upon a car,
So I could just say hi,
And my mum bought me a Mars bar
The man on the star said 'Why?'

I wish I had a robot,
So I could fly up at night,
And put a star in my pocket,
To use it as a special light.

I looked up again and saw a dash,
It was going round and round,
And then it made a flash,
But I caught it for a pound.

Adam Parkins (9)
Ridgeway Primary School

MR MAD THE INVENTOR

Mr Mad the inventor
Has hamsters that dance,
And flamingos that prance.

He makes his machines so wacky and weird,
He's even got one that can chop off a beard.

He's got a potion to go in slow motion,
What will he think of next?

The rocket in there
Is more like a bear
He's made things you couldn't imagine.

His book of inventions
At school would get him detention.
What will he think of next?

Richard Sharman (9)
Ridgeway Primary School

NIBBLE OR DRIBBLE

Rabbits nibble,
Dogs dribble.

Mice creep,
Deer leap.

Horses clop,
Frogs hop.

Pelicans bring,
Birds sing.

Elephants thump,
Caterpillars hump.

Chicks flutter,
Rats scutter.

Snakes slide,
Tigers hide.

Cats paw,
Eagles soar,
Cheetahs lie in the sun,
But I run.

Hannah Surkitt-Parr (8)
Ridgeway Primary School

I HAVE A BEST FRIEND

I have a best friend,
She has dark brown hair
She has hazel eyes
Also she has gold earrings.
She has a big brother called Adam
And a little sister called Katy.
I have a best friend.

I have a best friend
She has dark black hair
She comes from Scotland
She has a little brother called Ross
He is in Mrs May's Class.
He has broken his leg two times.
Her hair is always up,
She is always wearing a ring
I have a best friend.

I have a best friend,
She has light brown hair,
She has a big brother called Sam,
She wears school uniform
She goes to Ridgeway School.

Roxanne Gomez (8)
Ridgeway Primary School

THE EXPLORER'S ATTIC

In the dark wild attic of the explorer
Ancient bones of dinosaurs and people
Lie on the grey soil floor.

Hanging on the wall
Cobwebs as silver as the moon
On a dark night.

Falling apart books as old as can be
The Vikings did read them
Gosh they were older than you and me!

The smells are as if mummy's cloth has filled the room,
And rotted soil pongs in there,
Never go near if you feel queer.

There are no sounds except the antique wind chime,
Which has been around a very long time.

Creepy tombs from Egypt with bodies inside
They'll come alive if they want to,
They've got nothing to hide.

Ghostly wind is near,
Which only
King and Queen ghosts can hear.

Laura Brown (10)
Ridgeway Primary School

CLUTTER OF CHILDREN

There's a clutter of children every day,
Because they're all going out to play.
Our teacher is always cross,
Because she thinks she's the big boss.

The cloakroom's really small
It's like the teachers don't care at all.
We can't get our coats off,
So everybody will cough, cough, cough.

Everyone just loves break,
So they can have their double take.
Some children always play tig,
But the older kids just think they're big.

In the classroom we all like art,
But not when we get put apart.
We played four in a row,
So we all have to go with the flow.

The clutter of children come out of school,
And all head for the swimming pool.
Back tomorrow they will come
It's the clutter of children that's
    Everyone!

Nadine Dilley (9)
Ridgeway Primary School

SOAR AND ROAR

Donkeys kick
Cats lick.

Horses clop
Bunnies hop.

Eagles soar
Cheetahs roar.

Sparrows glide
Pythons slide.

Mice scutter
Butterflies flutter.

Parrots lie
Flies fly.

Hounds race
Lions chase.

Leopards stalk,
But -
I walk.

Jamie Curzon (9)
Ridgeway Primary School

MY CAT

My pet cat is very soft,
She loves my toy teddy
Even though her fur goes in my mouth,
Now she ate a butterfly
My cat is young.

People say she is very cute,
She will go in my room
And go to sleep.
She is only three
My cat is young.

People like her,
My cat
She's cute
My cat
My cat is young.

Lots of people like her,
My cat
I really love her
So does my sister
My cat is young!

Jake Thompson (9)
Ridgeway Primary School

The Inventor's Workshop

In the bright colourful workshop
Stood the clever, barmy inventor mixing a
Bubbly green potion.
Tools rattled as if there was an earthquake.
Wacky inventions jerked and wobbled
Frantically as if they were breaking down
As soon as they started.
The only sounds were the potions
Bubbling away so loud it sounded like it was
About to explode.
There was a smoky sweet smell in the old, stale air.
Cogs turned and squeaked as loud as a scream.
Complicated instructions fluttered about the room
Like a huge flock of birds trying to escape.
Long, coiled rope hung on the flaky walls.
Dusty old metal rolled gently in the soft breeze.
The only sounds were the potions bubbling away.

Abigail Jagoe (9)
Ridgeway Primary School

Pets

Pets are fun,
You can play with them every day
They always roll in the sun
Pets are fun.

Pets are fluffy
But they sometimes scratch you
They run and run and get happy
Pets are fluffy.

Pets are great
Sometimes it sleeps with me
But mostly it sleeps on slate
Pets are great.

Pets are greedy
They want to rule the land
They always listen to the same CD
Pets are greedy.

Nathan Saggers (8)
Ridgeway Primary School

THE BIG BAD VIKINGS

Vikings are dangerous,
Vikings are tough,
Vikings aren't generous,
But they are rough.
Don't mess with Vikings cause you'll get beat up,
Remember the Vikings, they raided us.

Remember the Vikings,
They fight with swords, bow and arrows,
But I wonder who was their Lord.
They would probably give the Romans a fright.
They had long beards,
Not like the people here.
Good job we're not Vikings,
Big, bad, fierce, human killing machines.

If they were here we would be dead,
But we are lucky without the Vikings.

Steven Jones (8)
Ridgeway Primary School

A Crazy Inventor's Workshop

In the inventor's workshop
Things toot, wacky machines hoot.

In the corner, a dirty great room
Tidier is crashing.
A red-hot grill is spitting fire,
Old wobbly test tubes are bubbling
And exploding chocolates are popping.

A strange wailing transporter is hovering above the ground,
Below there is a strange, whizzing sound.
A wet, wacky haircut machine is snipping,
And rats on the floor are nipping.

A splintery, tall workbench is rotting away,
The person who made these has work and no play.
The place smells of gas and smoke,
It makes me very nearly want to choke.

And then it goes quiet . . .
Until the laser beam starts flickering
And the metal starts clanging
Nails are strewn over the floor.

Then it goes quiet
Then it goes quiet,
Then it goes quiet.

George Sykes (9)
Ridgeway Primary School

CHOCOLATE MANIAC

I've got a sister she's a chocolate maniac.
I've got a Mum, she's chocolate insaniac.
I've got a Dad, well about him,
He hates chocolate,
He threw his in the bin.
Dad's too busy fixing the car.
I'm learning all about the stars.
Chocolate, chocolate that's not me
But my sister would jump for glee.
I've got a sister she's a chocolate maniac,
I've got a Mum she's chocolate insaniac.
I've got a Dad, well about him.
He hates chocolate,
He threw his in the bin.
My sister stuffs chocolate down her nose.
She tried to stuff it down the hose.
For puddings at dinner, I have plums.
But for Sophie and Mum it's choccy lumps.
I've got a sister she's a chocolate maniac,
I've got a Mum she's a chocolate insaniac.
I've got a Dad, well about him
He hates chocolate,
He threw his in the bin.
That's the end of the chocolate story.
So go back to your lives that are probably boring.

Hannah Williams (8)
Ridgeway Primary School

PETS!

I have a rabbit, it is very fluffy,
In a bundle of hay.
All snuggle down and warm
She jumps off my knee
And bites holes in my shorts,
Even my trousers.
I don't know how she does it
But she does it.
Sometimes she's naughty, sometimes she's good.
I love my rabbit as much as my family.
She's like a friend and a toy
She likes it with me.
She makes me happy when I'm sad
Is she one or is she two?
Very warm and very cuddly.
I think she gets scared in the dark.
Some nights warm, some nights cold,
Not going to get bigger because she's a dwarf.
By and by she will get older every year.
Not very friendly not at all.
Getting better by the minute.
One this year
Next year two
Very grey white as well.
Ears go up, ears go down.
In my hands in my fingers.
She stays in her cage day and night
In the dark and wet.

Sam Burgess (8)
Ridgeway Primary School

MY PERFECT PET

Not, one that wees in the kitchen,
Not, one that doesn't play,
Not, one that can't speak
I want an Elefisha Mutchen
Or an Aliena Fishalay.

But now I want a pet
That can jump, hop and leap,
That, can walk instead of crawl,
That, can squawk instead of speak.
I want a Monkephant
Or a Wuffalump.

No, now I want a pet that
Will, catch criminals,
Will, pounce at random,
Will, guard my treasure,
I want a Pagalon
Or a Dogon.

No actually I want a quiet pet that
Would sleep on my bed,
Would purr when I stroke
Would like lots of fuss.
I want an Astrososaurus.
O the perfect pet for me is a cat!

Joshua Allsopp (9)
Ridgeway Primary School

MY LOVEABLE CAT!

My cat is so loveable
All cuddly and warm,
As soft as you can imagine
He fills my heart with love not fear
My loveable cat.

My cat is ticklish under the chin
Sometimes you can see him giving a cattish grin,
I love my cat so much and if he ran away
I would sit down and pray for him
To come back this very day.

My loveable cat
Oh! He has scratched me once. Yes!
He was in a mood that day
And when we sat down together
He put his paw on my arm and
His other paw on my leg.

Just then he stretched out his claws
Then he dug in (ouch!)
It didn't hurt
I still love my cat though.
My Loveable Cat!

Raphaelle March (8)
Ridgeway Primary School

MY PET HAMSTER

I'm feeling rather lonely
So I remember my pet
I walked up the stairs
I saw him in his nice warm bed.

He wakes up and walks to the bars,
I try to pick him up,
He nibbles my hands,
So I leave him to settle.

I come back again,
He's calmed down.
But this time I think I should open
Him the other way.

He's very lively,
But that's at night-time.
I saw him do the monkey bars,
I don't know why he does them?

Polly Underwood (8)
Ridgeway Primary School

SWIMMING

S   mooth water
W ater is warm
I   n I jump
M oving quickly
M edals shining
I   love swimming
N ever be disappointed
G o and sing the National Anthem.

Bethany Gresley-Jones (7)
St Mary's CE Primary School, Melton Mowbray

RUNNING

R unning faster and faster
U ncertain that I am going to win my race
N ice and easy as I go
N earer and nearer to the finish line I get
I   am about to overtake
N ear the finish line now
G oing for Gold.

Lauren Sinnott (8)
St Mary's CE Primary School, Melton Mowbray

HORSES

H orses are fast
O ff we go
R iding is fun
S top we're at the end
E very second counts.

Sara Hall (7)
St Mary's CE Primary School, Melton Mowbray

MEDALS

All the stress to keep the boat going
Push and pull back and forward fast, fast, fast
I've just got it and I'm over the moon with myself,
I keep playing it over and over again in my head it's great!
I keep kissing my medal I feel great,
Waving at me from the crowd,
I'm really, really proud!
I love the crowd!

Annabelle Saxby (8)
St Mary's CE Primary School, Melton Mowbray

SWIMMING

S wimmers swim as fast as they can
W aves go up and down
I ce cold water
M y friends are cheering
M y heart is thumping
I magine your happy dreams
N ever panic when you're left behind
G old medal is good for me.

Megan Tymanskyj (8)
St Mary's CE Primary School, Melton Mowbray

THE VOYAGER

The Voyager is a wonderful ship
But now it's time to sail
I say goodbye to mother and father,
And climb aboard the ship.

The Voyager has set sail
Bobbing up and down,
The crew are drinking ale,
And I'm below the deck.

Night has fell,
Everyone is asleep,
The sea is calm and gentle,
Rocking me to sleep.

The morning's here,
We're up bright and early,
I'm washing the deck
The sun is shining bright.

Ellie Stapleton (11)
The Grove Primary School

A WONDERFUL RIVER

The wonderful river is as sparkly
As early morning dew.
The river goes around
Lots of bends
Not knowing where
He's going to end.
The river is so peaceful
Moving from place to place
I wish I were like the river
Or do I . . .?

Sophie Agar (10)
The Grove Primary School

WHAT AM I?

I like to wriggle like a snake
But I never like the chance to take,
A bite 'cause I don't need it,
I never breathe a bit.

I float like a feather,
I don't need to rely on the weather,
People can't see me or stare,
Because I am . . .?

Answer - Air.

Jennifer Sharp (11)
The Grove Primary School

THE RIVER'S VOYAGE

One cold and frozen day
The river went his usual way
How is he so frozen cold,
He can't stroll
Can he?
People think he's rough and clear
But really he's a gentle deer.
He flows and flows to seas and lakes
But really he's like a snake.
The river's voyage will be near an end
Or will it end?

Lilith Dickinson (11)
The Grove Primary School

THE RIVER

The river has not an end
Not a start.
It has no lungs and not a heart.
It does not smile, it does not frown,
It doesn't breathe,
It doesn't drown.
It does not think, it doesn't fly.
It does not eat,
It doesn't die.
As the children watch it swish and sway
The river's finished its job today.

Hannah Tatnell (9)
The Grove Primary School

FLYING WITH FANTASY

Flying with fairies,
So far so good.
Flying with fairies,
Don't fall in the mud.

Flying with Pegasus,
No gift from above.
Flying with Pegasus,
Like a white dove.

Flying with angels,
I would just love.
Flying with angels,
And floating above.

Amie-Leigh Claricoats (11)
The Grove Primary School

GRAN AND ME

Gran sits in her rocking chair,
She smiles at me
She puts her hands on her lap,
And calls me to sit with her.
I get on the rocking chair,
She hugs me tight.
I blow her a kiss
As I walk up the stairs,
I can't wait for tomorrow
When I see her again.

Catherine Bloxam (9)
The Grove Primary School

FOUR SEASONS

In comes spring,
Rainy days,
March, April
And May.

Then there's summer,
Lovely hot days,
On the beach,
You can see the waves.

Autumn is here,
Time for conker fights,
Getting ready for,
Dark, cold nights.

And then comes winter,
The dark nights have come,
The snow is here and
We're all having fun.

Gracie Ellam (10)
The Grove Primary School